\

Blueprint *of* God

By B. K. Uallah

Published by

R. B. Alfred aka B. K. Uallah

Queens New York 11413

Published by

B. K. Uallah

Publisher and distributor

Of

Blueprint *of* God

ISBN-13:

978-0615873510 (R.B. Alfred aka B.K. Uallah)

ISBN-10:

0615873510

Preface

I would like this book to simplify why God had to come from the direction of the east to the West in finding his people, who were put into bondage "Four hundred years". God has given all nations who needed a prophet, a messenger. For the people who were in "bondage" for "four hundred" years had to have one as well, since they never received one; after they had been brought into this strange land that is not ruled by their own people. Allah would take one from among "us" within that nation and give him wisdom so he can teach his people. Moses was taught by the scientist that a prophet would be similar to him that would be brought forth. The Scientist did not give any name but you can tell by the scripture that the prophecy is related to Elijah Muhammad.

Abraham also was told by the scientist his seeds would sojourn in a land that is not theirs and would go through "four hundred" years of miseducation, wrong kind of foods, and the inability to speak their own language and see things for themselves. Not wanting to hear anything from anyone saved the slave master. He would see everything from the perspective of his master. The lessons says "He likes the devil because the devil taught him how to eat the wrong food." This gave him an inability to recognize the truth of all things.

God would come at the end and bring the knowledge of the earth and heavens and all the measurements and distance of the planets from the sun. The Scientist explains this in the Bible, because they could foresee the future of our existence before it actually happens. And now we are going through that history and we cannot tell that it is us that this is relating to. This is why the lesson and the Holy Qur'an say, "Blind, deaf and dumb." We were made like that because the devil couldn't give self-knowledge to us if he wanted to make slaves out of us, so the devil took our names and called us by his names, and took away our true history and culture. He never taught us that we had ancient civilization. Thus, we lacked self-knowledge. A people that is made blind, deaf and dumb on purpose by their slave masters, so they could not recognize any Messiah who would come to save them.

Although, the scientist did not name America by name, but you can actually use mathematics to figure it out that it is America that is spoken of. America is the strongest country or nation on the earth. Wouldn't the wise scientist see a strong country like that in their predictions if they had supreme knowledge of such prediction? They really did not have to put every detail in the book, since it was a law for this to happen and it did happen. We are here after ***four hundred*** years and Elijah taught of the coming of God. He is the only one who fits the description of the Lamb. It was predicted that we would have a Messenger appointed to us in the Day of Ressurection or the terrible day of the Lord, which is what you call "the Last Days". This is not a time for prophet, yet it is a time for sunlight. Days of prophets where limited to moonlight in a dark place, but this is the seventh day, which represents thousands. This is why you must observe and keep the Sabbath holy. Christian, Jews and Sunni Muslims do not know what all this means. These are times for separation. For God came to separate us from our enemies. We do have enemies and even Martin Luther King, Jr. knew that. He said, "America gave us a bad check with insufficient funds". What do you think that meant? He was speaking on broken promises. He even tried to make us "Love" our "Enemies". But the only people who loves their enemies are the foolish so-called American Negroes. That is due to a lack of knowledge of yourself and your enemies. But now you are your own enemy, you can educate yourself now since God is present and we are a nation, God and earths. I side with the teachings of God. Like I said, the scientist did not mention America by name, but you can see it today as scientist saw it yesterday, and we shall come out with great substance. And this is why it says, "And he shall turn the heart of the fathers to the children, and the heart of the children to their fathers, lest I come and smite the earth with a curse." (Malachi 4:6).

"Behold, I will send you *Elijah the prophet* before the coming of the great and dreadful day of the *Lord*:" --Malachi 4:5.

Thus, you have the Messenger by name. Who taught Elijah? What direction did he come? How long ago? What year? What do you know about the teacher of Elijah? Did Jesus know about Elijah? Did Abraham know about Elijah? Did Moses know? Did Jacob know? If you want to know about yesterday you have to know what is going on today. Our situation was predicted in the Days of Abraham, Moses and Jesus; this was 4000 years after Moses, and two thousand years after Jesus, which is six thousand years? Thus, it goes back to the Great Pyramid and the knowledge is in there. The calculations (measurements) of the Pyramid explains the dates of our lessons, such as six thousand years and 281 verses in the second chapter in the Qur'an speaking of the children of Israel. Well, let us begin the chapters of the book and deal with the high science of our positions on the earth. This knowledge is very real and easy to understand, and this is why you were given or appointed a Messenger that will make you understand the very nature of all things in the universe, which is the correct knowledge. And we have to be thankful that Father Allah came to give us the lessons. They are not Muslim lessons, but they were lessons to uplift the black men in the wilderness of North America, whether you are Jew, Christian, Muslim or any persuasion that claim.

Table of Contents

Acknowledgement

This book is for anyone having the well-being of the black family at heart and sensitive to the pain and suffering of our people. Many of us have become so harden in our hearts, so cold that we see the suffering of the black family and are not affected by it. We have become a people outside the realm of Noah's ark, where it's drunkenness and confusion of the day. We have to climb off that stage of life and stop making excuses for our wrong doings. You are weak and have no strength to climb off that stage, because you are an actor. You are but a drunk trying to play God. It's real and you will get upset by the truth. The truth is the power so get mad. You are only fooling your own-self.

What is your own-self? Allah told us that we are God and not to let anyone tell us that we aren't Allah. Thus, we have to show and prove. And this goes for everyone. I'm speaking to the human families of the planet earth; Black, brown, yellow and white. No discrimination in the teachings and there is no compulsion in religion. For this is not a religion, but a way of God, which is the culture called by us Islam. Islam as we teach is the science of mathematics and means peace. This is our universal greeting. Peace is also the absence of all confusion. When one says "Peace", he is absent of all the spooky teachings of the Christians and Jews; and comes in the Name of Allah. Yet, if he is a Jew or Christian, let him have the proper understanding that can make him God. Like I said, there is no compulsion in religion like the Qur'an advocates. We are showing and proving divine culture. This is why it hurts me some of you are claiming knowledge of self and are still lost, and behave like destroy refinements (85%). You have not stop hating, being jealous, lusting and being greedy. You do not know how to treat your brother as an equal. In fact, you do not even treat your own brother from your mother like that; so you say, ". . . why should I treat someone else who says he is my brother like a brother?" This knowledge is realistic.

Basically, those who are conscious are happy to have their brother represents them and teach the sciences of life. A conscious man has civilization.

So, he does not have ill-will towards his brother. You all understand the lessons. Those lacking understanding of the lessons just hate, since they have nothing on brain. They, like the devil, condemn everything they do not understand. Why should one hate their own selves? That is like Cain and Abel in the Bible. Cain did not like that God accepted the offer made by Abel and Cain killed his brother for the purpose. So, we must get all the garbage off our mind and start building our nation. Allah said we are a nation and we refuse to see ourselves as a nation. You have people that are fewer in numbers (population) than we have, who calls themselves a nation, and here we are in America, 22 million strong and we do not call ourselves a nation. Allah called us a nation because he wanted for us to start working towards our independence like other people in this world. So, we are a nation within a nation. We do not use anything that the devil uses to build our civilization. There are people that have 1,000,000 people in population who are a nation. Well, that figure was in the 1930's, so the population must be more nowadays. It has not decreased, but they always keep the census of the black man in America a secret. They do not want us to know how filthy they are in their affairs. The devil keeps us blind to ourselves so he can master us. You'd be surprised how clever and cunning the devil is.

Genesis 3:1

King James Version (KJV)

Now the serpent was more subtil than any beast of the field which the Lord God had made. And he said unto the woman," Yea, hath God said, 'Ye shall not eat of every tree of the garden?'"

This was the same serpent that causes Eve to eat of the forbidden tree. The Bible makes the serpent more truthful than God, so how can the Bible be the book of God? *And the woman said unto the serpent, "We may eat of the fruit of the trees of the garden: But of the fruit of the tree which is in the midst of the garden, God hath said, 'Ye shall not eat of it, neither shall ye touch it, lest ye die.'"* (Genesis 3:2-3).

But then you see the devil at work, while you are not thinking of him he is at work, through the television, newspaper and his propaganda machines and trying to get you not to recognize your tree of knowledge, which is the root of civilization. So, the serpent said unto the woman, "Ye shall not surely die . . . For God doth know that in the day ye eat thereof, then your eyes shall be opened, and ye shall be as gods, knowing good and evil." Thus, the devil has used trick-knowledge to deceive Eve, and she went for it. Some of our woman has the Gods as such, where they allow the woman to control the relationship. The devil has been influencing some of our woman and you can see them on *Facebook* and programs as such. If they respected God as a black man they would not think about talking to God in disrespectful manners. Even some of the brothers who claim to be God also are under the influence of devils. Either that or they do not understand the lessons.

Who is that Prophet?

Everyone uses prophecy to prove the existence of their appointed messengers, so let us apply that same principles and show and prove that Elijah is the one called the ***Lamb*** and the one Jesus prophesized coming in the last days after departure from his disciples, who he called the "Comforter." It was not Muhammad of 1400 years ago, since he could not read or write, so he could not snatched the book from the hand of the one who sat on the throne in Revelation.

Revelation 5:1-14

King James Version (KJV)

And I saw in the right hand of him that sat on the throne a book written within and on the backside, sealed with seven seals . . . And I saw a strong angel proclaiming with a loud voice, Who is ***worthy*** to open the book, and to loose the seals thereof? And no man in heaven, nor in earth, neither under the earth, was able to open the book, neither to look thereon. . . And I wept much, because no man was found ***worthy*** to open ***and to read*** the book, neither to look thereon . . .And one of the elders saith unto me, Weep not: behold, the Lion of the tribe of Judah, the Root of David, hath prevailed to open the book, and to loose the seven seals thereof. . .***And I beheld***, and, lo, ***in the midst*** of the throne and of the four beasts, and in the midst of the elders, ***stood a Lamb as it had been slain***, having seven horns and seven eyes, which are the ***seven Spirits of God*** sent forth into all the earth. . . ***And he came and took the book out*** of the ***right hand of him*** that sat ***upon the throne***. . . And when he had taken the book, the four beasts and ***four*** and ***twenty elders fell down before the Lamb*** [24 scientist], having every one of them harps, and golden vials full of odours, which are the prayers of saints. . . And they sung a new song, saying, Thou art worthy to take the book, and to open the seals thereof: for thou wast slain, and hast redeemed us to God by thy blood out of every kindred, and tongue, and people, and nation; And hast made us unto our God kings and priests: and we shall reign on the earth. . . And I beheld, and I heard the voice of many angels round about the throne and the beasts and the elders: and the number of them was ten thousand times ten thousand, and thousands of thousands; Saying with a loud voice, Worthy is the Lamb that was slain to receive power, and riches, and wisdom, and strength, and honour, and glory, and blessing. . . And every creature which is in heaven, and on the earth, and under the earth, and such as are in the sea, and all that are in them, heard I saying, Blessing, and honour, and glory, and power, be unto him that sitteth upon the throne, and unto the Lamb for ever and ever. . . And the four beasts said, Amen. And the four and twenty elders fell down and worshipped him that liveth for ever and ever.

Elijah's name was changed due to the science that his name had to be changed and the name that he was given by the devils had to be left to the devils and God would give his servants their own name and the Bible bear witness to this. Thus, from Elijah Poole he was given the name Kareem Muhammad and then later gave him Elijah Muhammad, when he was given full duty of his position as a Messenger of the so-called American Negroes. But Muhammad means "Praised worthy" and Jesus mentions his name in the Qur'an. "And remember, Jesus, the son of Mary, said: 'O Children of Israel! I am the messenger of Allah (sent) to you, confirming the Law (which came) before me, and giving Glad Tidings of a Messenger to come after me, whose name shall be Ahmad.' But when he came to them with Clear Signs, they said, 'this is evident sorcery!'" (HQ. 61:6).

I am not saying that Muhammad 1400 years ago was not praiseworthy, but he was but a sign unto us. And the Qur'an bears witness to that. "Whatever is in the heavens and on earth, let it declare the Praises and Glory of Allah: for He is the Exalted in Might, the Wise." (HQ 61:1). Ahmad, according to Abdullah Yusuf Ali means, "Praised One"; and is "almost a translation of the Greek word *Periclytos*. In the present Gospel of John, xiv. 16, xv. 26; and xvi. 7, the word 'Comforter' in the English version is for the Greek word 'Paracletos', which means "Advocate", "one called to the help of another, a kind friend", rather than 'Comforter'." **Footnote: 5438**, (HQ. 61:6), by Abdullah Yusuf Ali. That could not have been talking about Muhammad ibn Abdullah of 1400 years ago. However, the proof lies in the transfiguration of Jesus Christ to his disciples in Matthew 17th.

1 ***After six days Jesus took with him Peter, James and John the brother of James, and led them up a high mountain by themselves.* 2 *There he was transfigured before them. His face shone like the sun, and his clothes became as white as the light.* 3 *Just then there appeared before them Moses and Elijah, talking with Jesus*.**

He gave the idea to his disciple who the "Comforter" would be, who would be a prophet like unto Moses. Moses was a prophet that came to separate and Muhammad came to integrate no matter what your life style was. All you had to do to be Muslim was to say that "I bear witness that Allah is God and that Muhammad is his Messenger". They call this in the Arabic words "Shahadah", which is the testimony of faith. Beside Muhammad could not read or write. He could not be the Lamb that would come in the Last Days. Jesus did not preach to Caucasians of his time, who were Greeks and Romans. However, after the transfiguration, which was an image or vision that Christ showed them, this is what the Bible says:

While he yet spake, behold, a bright cloud overshadowed them: and behold a voice out of the cloud, which said, "This is my beloved Son, in whom I am well pleased; hear ye him." And when the disciples heard it, they fell on their face, and were sore afraid . . . And Jesus came and touched them, and said, "Arise, and be not afraid" . . . And when they had lifted up their eyes, they saw no man, save Jesus only . . . And as they came down from the mountain, Jesus charged them, saying, "Tell the vision to no man, until the **Son of man** *be risen again from the dead" . . . And his disciples asked him, saying, "Why then say the scribes that Elias must first come?" And Jesus answered and said unto them, '***Elias*** *truly shall* **first come***, and* **restore all things**." (**Matthew 17:5-11**).

Jesus tells you by name that Elijah should first come and tell you "All truth and restore all things" and as the lessons say, "the science of everything in life". Will the Arabs and all the Muslim bear witness now? It is written and you say you believe in Allah's word, so do you see Elijah as you see your own son? However, we respect Prophet Muhammad 1400 years ago and he was but a sign for Elijah to come. He was prepared with no education, and illiterate, could not read or write, until one could snatch the book and break the seal thereof.

Yet every prophet had similar characteristics to Moses, but we are looking for a special one in the future that would be like Moses. Moses separated his people from Pharaoh. And God reminds you that he will send you Elijah in the Last Days or what he calls the *Days of Allah* or *Days of the Lord.*

***Remember ye the law of Moses my servant, which I commanded unto him in Horeb for all Israel, with the statutes and judgments . . . Behold, I will send you Elijah the prophet before the coming of the great and dreadful day of the Lord: And he shall turn the heart of the fathers to the children, and the heart of the children to their fathers, lest I come and smite the earth with a curse*.** (Malachi **4:4-6**), which means four thousand years after Moses, 400 years of bondage and within a Six thousand years period. It is all mathematically coded.

Even the Qur'an challenges the three major religions, by asking the entire world of faithful people or the total population of the planet; man, woman, and children:

Say: "***Do you see? Whether this message be from Allah, and yet you reject it, and a witness from among the Children of Israel bore witness of one like him*** . . ."

(HQ 46:10)

Muhammad 1400 years ago was made to say this, but this was not for him to address himself as that prophet, but someone to come. Even Muhammad said someone or Christ would come after him. He said: "The Knowledge (of when it will come) is only with Allah: I proclaim to you the mission on which I have been sent: But I see that ye are a people in ignorance!" . . . (HQ 46:23).

Deuteronomy 18:18

I will raise them up a Prophet from among their brethren, like unto thee, and will put my words in his mouth; and he shall speak unto them all that I shall command him.

Who is this speaking? God is speaking. And he knows the mind of the people whether you are Christian, Jew, Muslim or any other religious persuasion. He knows how disrespectful towards the truth you can be so he adds on to the above statements of verse 19th.

Deuteronomy 18:19

And it shall come to pass, that whosoever will not hearken unto my words which he shall speak in my name, I will require it of him.

Thus, you know it is hard to let go after you thought you had the whole truth and nothing but the truth; and truth has superseded your revelation. But righteous men bear witness to truth and righteousness. And this is the primal truth from God, who is the original man, the maker, the owner, cream of the planet earth and father of civilization. Did you ever wonder why Abraham did not deal with idols or that which does not speak or cannot help you in any form? Like the Holy Qur'an 48:28 say, "*Surely has Allah in truth fulfilled for His Messenger the Vision. You will certainly enter the Sacred Mosque, if Allah will, in security, some having their heads shaven, and others having their hair cut short; and you will have no fear. But He knew what you knew not. He has in fact ordained for you, besides that, a victory near at hand.*" **English Translation by Maulvi Sher Ali (ra).**

But Allah will tell you how to distinguish who his truthful prophets are. Not only Muhammad of 1400 years ago was a true prophet, but Elijah is also the true prophet, but he sees himself as a Messenger, because this is the Days of Allah, where you do not need prophets. Yet, he can be seen as the true and first prophet of the new world, which is Western civilization. God says:

"But the prophet, which shall presume to speak a word in my name, which I have not commanded him to speak, or that shall speak in the name of other gods, even that prophet shall die . . . And if thou say in thine heart, How shall we know the word which the Lord hath not spoken? When a prophet speaketh in the name of the Lord, if the thing follow not, nor come to pass, that is the thing which the Lord hath not spoken, but the prophet hath spoken it presumptuously: thou shalt not be afraid of him."

Elijah predicted the fall and declined of the dollar and it came to pass, and his teachings are still in accordance to the present and modern day. What was true yesterday should be true today, unless the truth of the matter is capable of changing. Like a child yesterday is a man today is truth, because we know that is the Law. But I have really proven that Elijah Muhammad is the one who was to be the Comforter of Jesus, called by name in the Bible and Holy Qur'an; but do not be too proud and deny him as such, if you say you respect God--Jews and Christians and Muslims. Abraham knew about us, since he was told by God himself that his seeds will become Imams in a strange land that is not theirs. 1 Thessalonians 5:21, says, "Prove ***all things***; hold fast that which is good."

Not only should you prove ***all things*** but you must "Study to shew thyself approved unto God, a workman that needeth not to be ashamed, rightly dividing the word of truth." (2 Timothy 2:15). However, Jesus also mentioned the "Comforter" in John 14:16:

"And I will pray the Father, and he shall give you another Comforter, that he may abide with you forever"

This is Jesus telling you about another, a different one from himself, not him, but one who will come after he is gone, who will teach his own people, like Jesus did. Like Moses; Jesus and Elijah Muhammad only taught their own people at first. Moses separated his people from the people of Pharaoh, Jesus told his disciples not to go into the ways of Gentiles or Samaritans. He called a Greek woman a dog or compared her to a dog. He called the white people devils, and whited sepulcher:

Matthew 23:27

" *Woe unto you, scribes and Pharisees, hypocrites! for ye are like unto whited sepulchres, which indeed appear beautiful outward, but are within full of dead men's bones, and of all uncleanness.*"

Elijah also called the white man the devil and history bears witness of them being devils. Gog and Magog is the people of the Caucasus Mountain. They oppose the laws of God, and seek to always change the Laws of God. He wants to make you think that marriage is legal between the same sexes, while God says a female was made for the male. Elijah said, "Babylon the great is fallen, is fallen, and is become the habitation of devils, and the hold of every foul spirit, and a cage of every unclean and hateful bird." (Revelation 18:2). Muhammad of 1400 years ago had no understanding of this and said that Allah only could tell you about what was to come. He was taught to quote but not to understand the sun-light. This is why he used moon-light to keep his calendar. He was given limited light, because it was not the Days of the Lord when he received his revelation. His people were not enslaved "*four hundred years*", but it would take the holy One from MT. Paran to come to the wilderness of North America, and today we see the prophecy by name, which Elijah says is "Modern Day Babylon".

If Gog and Magog were the Caucasians of yesterday, then you just look at today's Caucasians and see if they live parallel to each other to see if they are the same people. Gog and Magog opposed God yesterday, and the question is are they doing this today? Are Caucasians opposing God today? The lessons say, "He will not keep and obey the Laws" of the books, whether it is Bible or Qur'an and they use Jesus' name to justify their evil done on the earth, because they say they are not under the Law, but they are under Grace. You are always under the Law of God whether you acknowledge this or not. Today they are told not to eat pork, yet they say "Nothing God makes is Unclean" and "That was the Old Testament". Well, you say the Bible is the book of God, yet you show disrespect towards God if he says "Thou shall not eat the flesh of the swine, or touch of its carcase" and you claim "Nothing God makes is unclean". And the 85% believe in the devils on face value, which are known in the lesson as 10%. Is God a liar or the devil?

This is why the Son of man had to be raised from the east and select himself a messenger, so that he can teach his people who had to be raised. By that, I mean, he had to be risen so his people can also be raised, so they may be like him and have the knowledge of God. Why did he come to us? He knew the devil took everything from us and even our language. We had no knowledge in a strange land, and among strangers who did not care about righteousness, but were devils of the planet earth.

Hosea *4:6*

My people are destroyed for lack of knowledge:

Thus, God had to come himself and show us his ways and the Father had to pay close attention to Elijah and Malcolm X to learn all this and made his understanding Born or made manifested that he was Allah. And that is exactly who he was since Allah is the Arabic name for the Supreme Being and even Christ manifested that in his time. "Is it not written in your law, I said, Ye are gods?" (John 10:34) and Christ even went further by saying, "I and my Father are one." (John 10:30). He was taking them to, "I have said, 'Ye are gods; and all of you are children of the most High.'" (Psalms 82:6). Thus, there is nothing new about the black man being God and it is older than the sun, moon and stars. Pharaoh advocated they were God and they are one of the very first civilizations that existed at that time. Godfrey Higgins tells you that everything began in Egypt. The oldest statue in the world is the **Sphinx**, possessing a body of a lion and the face of a black man. That is the oldest proof of art work in the world. J.A. Rogers says it is 5,000 years of age. It is almost as old as Caucasians have been on the planet. They were in the caves when this was completed. However, do we have our prophet like unto Moses? It is Elijah in the bible and Muhammad in the Qur'an; both dealing with our Messenger, who has come to restore our people to their original selves. It is all calculated.

Are we the seeds of Abraham?

To know who the seeds of Abraham are we have to hear what God says and what is the effect of what God said; and Has the Bible quotes: come to pass? "**Know of surety**" meaning for sure you must "**know**" that "**your seeds**" shall be a "**Stranger**" in a land that is not "**theirs**". America is definitely not ours, although we have a black president, but look how much trouble the other politicians gives him. Even members of his own party did not respect his presidency. Hillary Clinton said, "Cain and I have experience, but Obama do not" and she was going against her own political party. Not only that, but she asked Obama to denounce Minister Louis Farrakhan. Why should he refute the minister when he is teaching the black people to live a righteous life? But that just shows you that they do not want you to come out with great substance. The devil wants to be your guide. He does not want you to know who you are, and she knows Farrakhan knows who black people are. We are the seeds of Abraham, from the tribe of Shabbazz. She (Hillary) is not going against her people. She knows her people are not with righteousness or the Laws of God.

Thus, if God wanted Abraham to know this, thus; the seeds had to know that as well. Face it. Why shouldn't the seeds know this knowledge? They were in bondage; they were mis-educated by the oppressor. So, they were destroyed for lack of self-knowledge. That nation which they shall serve will not give them the history of themselves; neither told them their origin in this world. They worshipped what they knew not and were easily lead in the wrong direction, but hard to be lead in the right directions. And it is all mathematical. Caucasians knew the science of this as well, but kept us blind to ourselves so he can master the original population of the earth. So he can master us and use us in his wars to gain him independence from his European fathers and rulers (England, the British Crown). It became close to our four hundred year cycle, but Abraham Lincoln allowed us physical deportation from his government, but we had no knowledge and had to depend on his administration for food, clothing and a home. If you have no knowledge and you are used to certain lifestyle how will you make a move on your own? You would have to be given knowledge. It was a crime for a black man to learn how to read. How could he go by himself with no knowledge? Does this answer the question of who the seeds of Abraham are? Abraham to Abraham Lincoln should be a sign to you all. It was 310 years that we have been in slavery, and we had nothing to build a civilization with. But on July 4, 1930 is when we obtained mental relief when Fard found us. Thus, W.D. Fard came after the abolishment of slavery in America, in 1865. But the English C. lesson 1-36 was written in 1934, because he said "379 years ago". Fard said, "He does not know he is my uncle." And some of you do not know you are his uncle, because you say he is white. His father is your brother, but no you want to throw everything the devil throw out there at us, because he does not want you to believe anything other than what he tells you. That is why he said, "He likes devil because the devil planted fear in him when he was a little boy". "He does not speak his own language." Why? Because he was taught to eat the wrong foods "Swine and Foods for thought". So, he speaks what was taught to him and this was not the teachings of the seeds of Abraham. He had to be given knowledge of himself. However, even after the four hundred years Allah taught: "*But in the fourth generation they shall come hither again: for the iniquity of the Amorites is not yet full.*" (Genesis 15:16). And you can tell that our problem is not political, not economical, but the lack of knowledge and our coming together as a nation.

Remember America came with a declaration of independence? Here is something about the creation of such constitution.

A More Perfect Union:

The Creation of the U.S. Constitution

May 25, 1787, Freshly spread dirt covered the cobblestone street in front of the Pennsylvania State House, protecting the men inside from the sound of passing carriages and carts. Guards stood at the entrances to ensure that the curious were kept at a distance. Robert Morris of Pennsylvania, the "financier" of the Revolution, opened the proceedings with a nomination--Gen. George Washington for the presidency of the Constitutional Convention. The vote was unanimous. With characteristic ceremonial modesty, the general expressed his embarrassment at his lack of qualifications to preside over such an august body and apologized for any errors into which he might fall in the course of its deliberations.

To many of those assembled, especially to the small, boyish-looking, 36-year-old delegate from Virginia, James Madison, the general's mere presence boded well for the convention, for the illustrious Washington gave to the gathering an air of importance and legitimacy But his decision to attend the convention had been an agonizing one. The Father of the Country had almost remained at home.

Suffering from rheumatism, despondent over the loss of a brother, absorbed in the management of Mount Vernon, and doubting that the convention would accomplish very much or that many men of stature would attend, Washington delayed accepting the invitation to attend for several months. Torn between the hazards of lending his reputation to a gathering perhaps doomed to failure and the chance that the public would view his reluctance to attend with a critical eye, the general finally agreed to make the trip. James Madison was pleased.

General George Washington was unanimously elected president of the Philadelphia convention.

The Articles of Confederation

The determined Madison had for several years insatiably studied history and political theory searching for a solution to the political and economic dilemmas he saw plaguing America. The Virginian's labors convinced him of the futility and weakness of confederacies of independent states. America's own government under the Articles of Confederation, Madison was convinced, had to be replaced. In force since 1781, established as a "league of friendship" and a constitution for the 13 sovereign and independent states after the Revolution, the articles seemed to Madison woefully inadequate. With the states retaining considerable power, the central government, he believed, had insufficient power to regulate commerce. It could not tax and was generally impotent in setting commercial policy It could not effectively support a war effort. It had little power to settle quarrels between states. Saddled with this weak government, the states were on the brink of economic disaster. The evidence was overwhelming. Congress was attempting to function with a depleted treasury; paper money was flooding the country, creating extraordinary inflation--a pound of tea in some areas could be purchased for a tidy $100; and the depressed condition of business was taking its toll on many small farmers. Some of them were being thrown in jail for debt, and numerous farms were being confiscated and sold for taxes.

In 1786 some of the farmers had fought back. Led by Daniel Shays, a former captain in the Continental army, a group of armed men, sporting evergreen twigs in their hats, prevented the circuit court from sitting at Northampton, MA, and threatened to seize muskets stored in the arsenal at Springfield. Although the insurrection was put down by state troops, the incident confirmed the fears of many wealthy men that anarchy was just around the corner. Embellished day after day in the press, the uprising made upper-class Americans shudder as they imagined hordes of vicious outlaws descending upon innocent citizens. From his idyllic Mount Vernon setting, Washington wrote to Madison: "Wisdom and good examples are necessary at this time to rescue the political machine from the impending storm."

Madison thought he had the answer. He wanted a strong central government to provide order and stability. "Let it be tried then," he wrote, "whether any middle ground can be taken which will at once support a due supremacy of the national authority," while maintaining state power only when "subordinately useful." The resolute Virginian looked to the Constitutional Convention to forge a new government in this mold.

The convention had its specific origins in a proposal offered by Madison and John Tyler in the Virginia assembly that the Continental Congress be given power to regulate commerce throughout the Confederation. Through their efforts in the assembly a plan was devised inviting the several states to attend a convention at Annapolis, MD, in September 1786 to discuss commercial problems. Madison and a young lawyer from New York named Alexander Hamilton issued a report on the meeting in Annapolis, calling upon Congress to summon delegates of all of the states to meet for the purpose of revising the Articles of Confederation. Although the report was widely viewed as a usurpation of congressional authority, the Congress did issue a formal call to the states for a convention. To Madison it represented the supreme chance to reverse the country's trend. And as the delegations gathered in Philadelphia, its importance was not lost to others. The squire of Gunston Hall, George Mason, wrote to his son, "The Eyes of the United States are turned upon this Assembly and their Expectations raised to a very anxious Degree. May God Grant that we may be able to gratify them, by establishing a wise and just Government."

The Delegates

Seventy-four delegates were appointed to the convention, of which 55 actually attended sessions. Rhode Island was the only state that refused to send delegates. Dominated by men wedded to paper currency, low taxes, and popular government, Rhode Island's leaders refused to participate in what they saw as a conspiracy to overthrow the established government. Other Americans also had their suspicions. Patrick Henry, of the flowing red Glasgow cloak and the magnetic oratory, refused to attend, declaring he "smelt a rat." He suspected, correctly, that Madison had in mind the creation of a powerful central government and the subversion of the authority of the state legislatures. Henry along with many other political leaders, believed that the state governments offered the chief protection for personal liberties. He was determined not to lend a hand to any proceeding that seemed to pose a threat to that protection.

With Henry absent, with such towering figures as Jefferson and Adams abroad on foreign missions, and with John Jay in New York at the Foreign Office, the convention was without some of the country's major political leaders. It was, nevertheless, an impressive assemblage. In addition to Madison and Washington, there were Benjamin Franklin of Pennsylvania--crippled by gout, the 81-year-old Franklin was a man of many dimensions printer, storekeeper, publisher, scientist, public official, philosopher, diplomat, and ladies' man; James Wilson of Pennsylvania--a distinguished lawyer with a penchant for ill-advised land-jobbing schemes, which would force him late in life to flee from state to state avoiding prosecution for debt, the Scotsman brought a profound mind steeped in constitutional theory and law; Alexander Hamilton of New York--a brilliant, ambitious former aide-de-camp and secretary to Washington during the Revolution who had, after his marriage into the Schuyler family of New York, become a powerful political figure; George Mason of Virginia--the author of the Virginia Bill of Rights whom Jefferson later called "the Cato of his country without the avarice of the Roman"; John Dickinson of Delaware--the quiet, reserved author of the "Farmers' Letters" and chairman of the congressional committee that framed the articles; and Gouverneur Morris of Pennsylvania-- well versed in French literature and language, with a flair and bravado to match his keen intellect, who had helped draft the New York State Constitution and had worked with Robert Morris in the Finance Office.

There were others who played major roles - Oliver Ellsworth of Connecticut; Edmund Randolph of Virginia; William Paterson of New Jersey; John Rutledge of South Carolina; Elbridge Gerry of Massachusetts; Roger Sherman of Connecticut; Luther Martin of Maryland; and the Pinckneys, Charles and Charles Cotesworth, of South Carolina. Franklin was the oldest member and Jonathan Dayton, the 27-year-old delegate from New Jersey was the youngest. The average age was 42. Most of the delegates had studied law, had served in colonial or state legislatures, or had been in the Congress. Well versed in philosophical theories of government advanced by such philosophers as James Harrington, John Locke, and Montesquieu, profiting from experience gained in state politics, the delegates composed an exceptional body, one that left a remarkably learned record of debate. Fortunately we have a relatively complete record of the proceedings, thanks to the indefatigable James Madison. Day after day, the Virginian sat in front of the presiding officer, compiling notes of the debates, not missing a single day or a single major speech. He later remarked that his self-confinement in the hall, which was often oppressively hot in the Philadelphia summer, almost killed him.

The sessions of the convention were held in secret--no reporters or visitors were permitted. Although many of the naturally loquacious members were prodded in the pubs and on the streets, most remained surprisingly discreet. To those suspicious of the convention, the curtain of secrecy only served to confirm their anxieties. Luther Martin of Maryland later charged that the conspiracy in Philadelphia needed a quiet breeding ground. Thomas Jefferson wrote John Adams from Paris, "I am sorry they began their deliberations by so abominable a precedent as that of tying up the tongues of their members."

The Virginia Plan

On Tuesday morning, May 29, Edmund Randolph, the tall, 34-year- old governor of Virginia, opened the debate with a long speech decrying the evils that had befallen the country under the Articles of Confederation and stressing the need for creating a strong national government. Randolph then outlined a broad plan that he and his Virginia compatriots had, through long sessions at the Indian Queen tavern, put together in the days preceding the convention. James Madison had such a plan on his mind for years. The proposed government had three branches--legislative, executive, and judicial--each branch structured to check the other. Highly centralized, the government would have veto power over laws enacted by state legislatures. The plan, Randolph confessed, "meant a strong consolidated union in which the idea of states should be nearly annihilated." This was, indeed, the rat so offensive to Patrick Henry.

The introduction of the so-called Virginia Plan at the beginning of the convention was a tactical coup. The Virginians had forced the debate into their own frame of reference and in their own terms.

For 10 days the members of the convention discussed the sweeping and, too many delegates, startling Virginia resolutions. The critical issue, described succinctly by Gouverneur Morris on May 30, was the distinction between a federation and a national government, the "former being a mere compact resting on the good faith of the parties; the latter having a complete and compulsive operation." Morris favored the latter, a "supreme power" capable of exercising necessary authority not merely a shadow government, fragmented and hopelessly ineffective.

The New Jersey Plan

This nationalist position revolted many delegates who cringed at the vision of a central government swallowing state sovereignty. On June 13 delegates from smaller states rallied around proposals offered by New Jersey delegate William Paterson. Railing against efforts to throw the states into "hotchpot," Paterson proposed a "union of the States merely federal." The "New Jersey resolutions" called only for a revision of the articles to enable the Congress more easily to raise revenues and regulate commerce. It also provided that acts of Congress and ratified treaties be "the supreme law of the States."

For 3 days the convention debated Paterson's plan, finally voting for rejection. With the defeat of the New Jersey resolutions, the convention was moving toward creation of a new government, much to the dismay of many small-state delegates. The nationalists, led by Madison, appeared to have the proceedings in their grip. In addition, they were able to persuade the members that any new constitution should be ratified through conventions of the people and not by the Congress and the state legislatures- -another tactical coup. Madison and his allies believed that the constitution they had in mind would likely be scuttled in the legislatures, where many state political leaders stood to lose power. The nationalists wanted to bring the issue before "the people," where ratification was more likely.

Hamilton's Plan

On June 18 Alexander Hamilton presented his own ideal plan of government. Erudite and polished, the speech, nevertheless, failed to win a following. It went too far. Calling the British government "the best in the world," Hamilton proposed a model strikingly similar an executive to serve during good behavior or life with veto power over all laws; a senate with members serving during good behavior; the legislature to have power to pass "all laws whatsoever." Hamilton later wrote to Washington that the people were now willing to accept "something not very remote from that which they have lately quitted." What the people had "lately quitted," of course, was monarchy. Some members of the convention fully expected the country to turn in this direction. Hugh Williamson of North Carolina, a wealthy physician, declared that it was "pretty certain . . . that we should at some time or other have a king." Newspaper accounts appeared in the summer of 1787 alleging that a plot was under way to invite the second son of George III, Frederick, Duke of York, the secular bishop of Osnaburgh in Prussia, to become "king of the United States."

Alexander Hamilton on June 18 called the British government "the best in the world" and proposed a model strikingly similar. The erudite New Yorker, however, later became one of the most ardent spokesmen for the new Constitution.

Strongly militating against any serious attempt to establish monarchy was the enmity so prevalent in the revolutionary period toward royalty and the privileged classes. Some state constitutions had even prohibited titles of nobility. In the same year as the Philadelphia convention, Royall Tyler, a revolutionary war veteran, in his play The Contract, gave his own jaundiced view of the upper classes:

Exult each patriot heart! This night is shewn

A piece, which we may fairly call our own;

Where the proud titles of "My Lord!" "Your Grace!"

To humble Mr. and plain Sir give place.

Most delegates were well aware that there were too many Royall Tylers in the country, with too many memories of British rule and too many ties to a recent bloody war, to accept a king. As the debate moved into the specifics of the new government, Alexander Hamilton and others of his persuasion would have to accept something less.

By the end of June, debate between the large and small states over the issue of representation in the first chamber of the legislature was becoming increasingly acrimonious. Delegates from Virginia and other large states demanded that voting in Congress be according to population; representatives of smaller states insisted upon the equality they had enjoyed under the articles. With the oratory degenerating into threats and accusations, Benjamin Franklin appealed for daily prayers. Dressed in his customary gray homespun, the aged philosopher pleaded that "the Father of lights . . . illuminate our understandings." Franklin's appeal for prayers was never fulfilled; the convention, as Hugh Williamson noted, had no funds to pay a preacher.

On June 29 the delegates from the small states lost the first battle. The convention approved a resolution establishing population as the basis for representation in the House of Representatives, thus favoring the larger states. On a subsequent small-state proposal that the states have equal representation in the Senate, the vote resulted in a tie. With large-state delegates unwilling to compromise on this issue, one member thought that the convention "was on the verge of dissolution, scarce held together by the strength of an hair."

By July 10 George Washington was so frustrated over the deadlock that he bemoaned "having had any agency" in the proceedings and called the opponents of a strong central government "narrow minded politicians . . . under the influence of local views." Luther Martin of Maryland, perhaps one whom Washington saw as "narrow minded," thought otherwise. A tiger in debate, not content merely to parry an opponent's argument but determined to bludgeon it into eternal rest, Martin had become perhaps the small states' most effective, if irascible, orator. The Marylander leaped eagerly into the battle on the representation issue declaring, "The States have a right to an equality of representation. This is secured to us by our present articles of confederation; we are in possession of this privilege."

The Great Compromise

Also crowding into this complicated and divisive discussion over representation was the North-South division over the method by which slaves were to be counted for purposes of taxation and representation. On July 12 Oliver Ellsworth proposed that representation for the lower house be based on the number of free persons and three-fifths of "all other persons," a euphemism for slaves. In the following week the members finally compromised, agreeing that direct taxation be according to representation and that the representation of the lower house be based on the white inhabitants and three-fifths of the "other people." With this compromise and with the growing realization that such compromise was necessary to avoid a complete breakdown of the convention, the members then approved Senate equality. Roger Sherman had remarked that it was the wish of the delegates "that some general government should be established." With the crisis over representation now settled, it began to look again as if this wish might be fulfilled.

For the next few days the air in the City of Brotherly Love, although insufferably muggy and swarming with blue-bottle flies, had the clean scent of conciliation. In this period of welcome calm, the members decided to appoint a Committee of Detail to draw up a draft constitution. The convention would now at last have something on paper. As Nathaniel Gorham of Massachusetts, John Rutledge, Edmund Randolph, James Wilson, and Oliver Ellsworth went to work, the other delegates voted themselves a much needed 10-day vacation.

During the adjournment, Gouverneur Morris and George Washington rode out along a creek that ran through land that had been part of the Valley Forge encampment 10 years earlier. While Morris cast for trout, Washington pensively looked over the now lush ground where his freezing troops had suffered, at a time when it had seemed as if the American Revolution had reached its end. The country had come a long way.

The First Draft

On Monday August 6, 1787, the convention accepted the first draft of the Constitution. Here was the article-by-article model from which the final document would result some 5 weeks later. As the members began to consider the various sections, the willingness to compromise of the previous days quickly evaporated. The most serious controversy erupted over the question of regulation of commerce. The southern states, exporters of raw materials, rice, indigo, and tobacco, were fearful that a New England-dominated Congress might, through export taxes, severely damage the South's economic life. C. C. Pinckney declared that if Congress had the power to regulate trade, the southern states would be "nothing more than overseers for the Northern States."

On August 21 the debate over the issue of commerce became very closely linked to another explosive issue--slavery. When Martin of Maryland proposed a tax on slave importation, the convention was thrust into a strident discussion of the institution of slavery and its moral and economic relationship to the new government. Rutledge of South Carolina, asserting that slavery had nothing at all to do with morality, declared, "Interest alone is the governing principle with nations." Sherman of Connecticut was for dropping the tender issue altogether before it jeopardized the convention. Mason of Virginia expressed concern over unlimited importation of slaves but later indicated that he also favored federal protection of slave property already held. This nagging issue of possible federal intervention in slave traffic, which Sherman and others feared could irrevocably split northern and southern delegates, was settled by, in Mason's words, "a bargain." Mason later wrote that delegates from South Carolina and Georgia, who most feared federal meddling in the slave trade, made a deal with delegates from the New England states. In exchange for the New Englanders' support for continuing slave importation for 20 years, the southerners accepted a clause that required only a simple majority vote on navigation laws, a crippling blow to southern economic interests.

The bargain was also a crippling blow to those working to abolish slavery. Congregationalist minister and abolitionist Samuel Hopkins of Connecticut charged that the convention had sold out: "How does it appear . . . that these States, who have been fighting for liberty and consider themselves as the highest and most noble example of zeal for it, cannot agree in any political Constitution, unless it indulge and authorize them to enslave their fellow men . . . Ah! These unclean spirits, like frogs, they, like the Furies of the poets are spreading discord, and exciting men to contention and war." Hopkins considered the Constitution a document fit for the flames.

On August 31 a weary George Mason, who had 3 months earlier written so expectantly to his son about the "great Business now before us," bitterly exclaimed that he "would sooner chop off his right hand than put it to the Constitution as it now stands." Mason despaired that the convention was rushing to saddle the country with an ill-advised, potentially ruinous central authority He was concerned that a "bill of rights," ensuring individual liberties, had not been made part of the Constitution. Mason called for a new convention to reconsider the whole question of the formation of a new government. Although Mason's motion was overwhelmingly voted down, opponents of the Constitution did not abandon the idea of a new convention. It was futilely suggested again and again for over 2 years.

One of the last major unresolved problems was the method of electing the executive. A number of proposals, including direct election by the people, by state legislatures, by state governors, and by the national legislature, were considered. The result was the electoral college, a master stroke of compromise, quaint and curious but politically expedient. The large states got proportional strength in the number of delegates, the state legislatures got the right of selecting delegates, and the House the right to choose the president in the event no candidate received a majority of electoral votes. Mason later predicted that the House would probably choose the president 19 times out of 20.

In the early days of September, with the exhausted delegates anxious to return home, compromise came easily. On September 8 the convention was ready to turn the Constitution over to a Committee of Style and Arrangement. Gouverneur Morris was the chief architect. Years later he wrote to Timothy Pickering: "That Instrument was written by the Fingers which wrote this letter." The Constitution was presented to the convention on September 12, and the delegates methodically began to consider each section. Although close votes followed on several articles, it was clear that the grueling work of the convention in the historic summer of 1787 was reaching its end.

Before the final vote on the Constitution on September 15, Edmund Randolph proposed that amendments be made by the state conventions and then turned over to another general convention for consideration. He was joined by George Mason and Elbridge Gerry. The three lonely allies were soundly rebuffed. Late in the afternoon the roll of the states was called on the Constitution, and from every delegation the word was "Aye."

On September 17 the members met for the last time, and the venerable Franklin had written a speech that was delivered by his colleague James Wilson. Appealing for unity behind the Constitution, Franklin declared, "I think it will astonish our enemies, who are waiting with confidence to hear that our councils are confounded like those of the builders of Babel; and that our States are on the point of separation, only to meet hereafter for the purpose of cutting one another's throats." With Mason, Gerry, and Randolph withstanding appeals to attach their signatures, the other delegates in the hall formally signed the Constitution, and the convention adjourned at 4 o'clock in the afternoon.

Weary from weeks of intense pressure but generally satisfied with their work, the delegates shared a farewell dinner at City Tavern. Two blocks away on Market Street, printers John Dunlap and David Claypoole worked into the night on the final imprint of the six-page Constitution, copies of which would leave Philadelphia on the morning stage. The debate over the nation's form of government was now set for the larger arena.

As the members of the convention returned home in the following days, Alexander Hamilton privately assessed the chances of the Constitution for ratification. In its favor were the support of Washington, commercial interests, men of property, creditors, and the belief among many Americans that the Articles of Confederation were inadequate. Against it were the opposition of a few influential men in the convention and state politicians fearful of losing power, the general revulsion against taxation, the suspicion that a centralized government would be insensitive to local interests, and the fear among debtors that a new government would "restrain the means of cheating Creditors."

The Federalists and the Anti-Federalists

Because of its size, wealth, and influence and because it was the first state to call a ratifying convention, Pennsylvania was the focus of national attention. The positions of the Federalists, those who supported the Constitution, and the anti-Federalists, those who opposed it, were printed and reprinted by scores of newspapers across the country. And passions in the state were most warm. When the Federalist-dominated Pennsylvania assembly lacked a quorum on September 29 to call a state ratifying convention, a Philadelphia mob, in order to provide the necessary numbers, dragged two anti-Federalist members from their lodgings through the streets to the State House where the bedraggled representatives were forced to stay while the assembly voted. It was a curious example of participatory democracy.

On October 5 anti-Federalist Samuel Bryan published the first of his "Centinel" essays in Philadelphia's Independent Gazetteer. Republished in newspapers in various states, the essays assailed the sweeping power of the central government, the usurpation of state sovereignty, and the absence of a bill of rights guaranteeing individual liberties such as freedom of speech and freedom of religion. "The United States are to be melted down," Bryan declared, into a despotic empire dominated by "well-born" aristocrats. Bryan was echoing the fear of many anti-Federalists that the new government would become one controlled by the wealthy established families and the culturally refined. The common working people, Bryan believed, were in danger of being subjugated to the will of an all-powerful authority remote and inaccessible to the people. It was this kind of authority, he believed, that Americans had fought a war against only a few years earlier.

The next day James Wilson, delivering a stirring defense of the Constitution to a large crowd gathered in the yard of the State House, praised the new government as the best "which has ever been offered to the world." The Scotsman's view prevailed. Led by Wilson, Federalists dominated in the Pennsylvania convention, carrying the vote on December 12 by a healthy 46 to 23.

The vote for ratification in Pennsylvania did not end the rancor and bitterness. Franklin declared that scurrilous articles in the press were giving the impression that Pennsylvania was "peopled by a set of the most unprincipled, wicked, rascally and quarrelsome scoundrels upon the face of the globe." And in Carlisle, on December 26, anti-Federalist rioters broke up a Federalist celebration and hung Wilson and the Federalist chief justice of

Pennsylvania, Thomas McKean, in effigy; put the torch to a copy of the Constitution; and busted a few Federalist heads.

In New York the Constitution was under siege in the press by a series of essays signed "Cato." Mounting a counterattack, Alexander Hamilton and John Jay enlisted help from Madison and, in late 1787; they published the first of a series of essays now known as the Federalist Papers. The 85 essays, most of which were penned by Hamilton himself, probed the weaknesses of the Articles of Confederation and the need for an energetic national government. Thomas Jefferson later called the Federalist Papers the "best commentary on the principles of government ever written."

Against this kind of Federalist leadership and determination, the opposition in most states was disorganized and generally inert. The leading spokesmen were largely state-centered men with regional and local interests and loyalties. Madison wrote of the Massachusetts anti-Federalists, "There was not a single character capable of uniting their wills or directing their measures. . . . They had no plan whatever." The anti-Federalists attacked wildly on several fronts: the lack of a bill of rights, discrimination against southern states in navigation legislation, direct taxation, the loss of state sovereignty. Many charged that the Constitution represented the work of aristocratic politicians bent on protecting their own class interests. At the Massachusetts convention one delegate declared, "These lawyers, and men of learning and moneyed men, that . . . make us poor illiterate people swallow down the pill . . . they will swallow up all us little folks like the great Leviathan; yes, just as the whale swallowed up Jonah!" Some newspaper articles, presumably written by anti-Federalists, resorted to fanciful predictions of the horrors that might emerge under the new Constitution pagans and deists could control the government; the use of Inquisition-like torture could be instituted as punishment for federal crimes; even the pope could be elected president.

One anti-Federalist argument gave opponents some genuine difficulty--the claim that the territory of the 13 states was too extensive for a representative government. In a republic embracing a large area, anti-Federalists argued, government would be impersonal, unrepresentative, dominated by men of wealth, and oppressive of the poor and working classes. Had not the illustrious Montesquieu himself ridiculed the notion that an extensive territory composed of varying climates and people, could be a single republican state? James Madison, always ready with the Federalist volley, turned the argument completely around and insisted that the vastness of the country would itself be a strong argument in favor of a republic. Claiming that a large republic would counterbalance various political interest groups vying for power, Madison wrote, "The smaller the society the fewer probably will be the distinct parties and interests composing it; the fewer the distinct parties and interests, the more frequently will a majority be found of the same party and the more easily will they concert and execute their plans of oppression." Extend the size of the republic, Madison argued, and the country would be less vulnerable to separate factions within it.

Ratification

By January 9, 1788, five states of the nine necessary for ratification had approved the Constitution--Delaware, Pennsylvania, New Jersey, Georgia, and Connecticut. But the eventual outcome remained uncertain in pivotal states such as Massachusetts, New York, and Virginia. On February 6, with Federalists agreeing to recommend a list of amendments amounting to a bill of rights, Massachusetts ratified by a vote of 187 to 168. The revolutionary leader, John Hancock, elected to preside over the Massachusetts ratifying convention but unable to make up his mind on the Constitution, took to his bed with a convenient case of gout. Later seduced by the Federalists with visions of the vice presidency and possibly the presidency, Hancock, whom Madison noted as "an idolater of popularity," suddenly experienced a miraculous cure and delivered a critical block of votes. Although Massachusetts was now safely in the Federalist column, the recommendation of a bill of rights was a significant victory for the anti-Federalists. Six of the remaining states later appended similar recommendations.

When the New Hampshire convention was adjourned by Federalists who sensed imminent defeat and when Rhode Island on March 24 turned down the Constitution in a popular referendum by an overwhelming vote of 10 to 1, Federalist leaders were apprehensive. Looking ahead to the Maryland convention, Madison wrote to Washington, "The difference between even a postponement and adoption in Maryland may . . . possibly give a fatal advantage to that which opposes the constitution." Madison had little reason to worry. The final vote on April 28 63 for, 11 against. In Baltimore, a huge parade celebrating the Federalist victory rolled through the downtown streets, highlighted by a 15-foot float called "Ship Federalist." The symbolically seaworthy craft was later launched in the waters off Baltimore and sailed down the Potomac to Mount Vernon.

On July 2, 1788, the Confederation Congress, meeting in New York, received word that a reconvened New Hampshire ratifying convention had approved the Constitution. With South Carolina's acceptance of the Constitution in May, New Hampshire thus became the ninth state to ratify. The Congress appointed a committee "for putting the said Constitution into operation."

In the next 2 months, thanks largely to the efforts of Madison and Hamilton in their own states, Virginia and New York both ratified while adding their own amendments. The margin for the Federalists in both states, however, was extremely close. Hamilton figured that the majority of the people in New York actually opposed the Constitution, and it is probable that a majority of people in the entire country opposed it. Only the promise of amendments had ensured a Federalist victory.

The Bill of Rights

The call for a bill of rights had been the anti-Federalists' most powerful weapon. Attacking the proposed Constitution for its vagueness and lack of specific protection against tyranny, Patrick Henry asked the Virginia convention, "What can avail your specious, imaginary balances, your rope-dancing, chain-rattling, ridiculous ideal checks and contrivances." The anti-Federalists, demanding a more concise, unequivocal Constitution, one that laid out for all to see the right of the people and limitations of the power of government, claimed that the brevity of the document only revealed its inferior nature. Richard Henry Lee despaired at the lack of provisions to protect "those essential rights of mankind without which liberty cannot exist." Trading the old government for the new without such a bill of rights, Lee argued, would be trading Scylla for Charybdis.

A bill of rights had been barely mentioned in the Philadelphia convention, most delegates holding that the fundamental rights of individuals had been secured in the state constitutions. James Wilson maintained that a bill of rights was superfluous because all power not expressly delegated to thenew government was reserved to the people. It was clear, however, that in this argument the anti-Federalists held the upper hand. Even Thomas Jefferson, generally in favor of the new government, wrote to Madison that a bill of rights was "what the people are entitled to against every government on earth."

By the fall of 1788 Madison had been convinced that not only was a bill of rights necessary to ensure acceptance of the Constitution but that it would have positive effects. He wrote, on October 17, that such "fundamental maxims of free Government" would be "a good ground for an appeal to the sense of community" against potential oppression and would "counteract the impulses of interest and passion."

Madison's support of the bill of rights was of critical significance. One of the new representatives from Virginia to the First Federal Congress, as established by the new Constitution, he worked tirelessly to persuade the House to enact amendments. Defusing the anti-Federalists' objections to the Constitution, Madison was able to shepherd through 17 amendments in the early months of the Congress, a list that was later trimmed to 12 in the Senate. On October 2, 1789, President Washington sent to each of the states a copy of the 12 amendments adopted by the Congress in September. By December 15, 1791, three-fourths of the states had ratified the 10 amendments now so familiar to Americans as the "Bill of Rights."

Benjamin Franklin told a French correspondent in 1788 that the formation of the new government had been like a game of dice, with many players of diverse prejudices and interests unable to make any uncontested moves. Madison wrote to Jefferson that the welding of these clashing interests was "a task more difficult than can be well conceived by those who were not concerned in the execution of it." When the delegates left Philadelphia after the convention, few, if any, were convinced that the Constitution they had approved outlined the ideal form of government for the country. But late in his life James Madison scrawled out another letter, one never addressed. In it he declared that no government can be perfect, and "that which is the least imperfect is therefore the best government."

The Document Enshrined

The fate of the United States Constitution after its signing on September 17, 1787, can be contrasted sharply to the travels and physical abuse of America's other great parchment, the Declaration of Independence. As the Continental Congress, during the years of the revolutionary war, scurried from town to town, the rolled-up

Declaration was carried along. After the formation of the new government under the Constitution, the one-page Declaration, eminently suited for display purposes, graced the walls of various government buildings in Washington, exposing it to prolonged damaging sunlight. It was also subjected to the work of early calligraphers responding to a demand for reproductions of the revered document. As any visitor to the National Archives can readily observe, the early treatment of the now barely legible Declaration took a disastrous toll. The Constitution, in excellent physical condition after more than 200 years, has enjoyed a more serene existence. By 1796 the Constitution was in the custody of the Department of State along with the Declaration and traveled with the federal government from New York to Philadelphia to Washington. Both documents were secretly moved to Leesburg, VA, before the imminent attack by the British on Washington in 1814. Following the war, the Constitution remained in the State Department while the Declaration continued its travels--to the Patent Office Building from 1841 to 1876, to Independence Hall in Philadelphia during the Centennial celebration, and back to Washington in 1877. On September 29, 1921, President Warren Harding issued an Executive order transferring the Constitution and the Declaration to the Library of Congress for preservation and exhibition. The next day Librarian of Congress Herbert Putnam, acting on authority of Secretary of State Charles Evans Hughes, carried the Constitution and the Declaration in a Model-T Ford truck to the library and placed them in his office safe until an appropriate exhibit area could be constructed. The documents were officially put on display at a ceremony in the library on February 28, 1924. On February 20, 1933, at the laying of the cornerstone of the future National Archives Building, President Herbert Hoover remarked, "There will be aggregated here the most sacred documents of our history--the originals of the Declaration of Independence and of the Constitution of the United States." The two documents however, were not immediately transferred to the Archives. During World War II both were moved from the library to Fort Knox for protection and returned to the library in 1944. It was not until successful negotiations were completed between Librarian of Congress Luther Evans and Archivist of the United States Wayne Grover that the transfer to the National Archives was finally accomplished by special direction of the Joint Congressional Committee on the Library.

On December 13, 1952, the Constitution and the Declaration were placed in helium-filled cases, enclosed in wooden crates, laid on mattresses in an armored Marine Corps personnel carrier, and escorted by ceremonial troops, two tanks, and four servicemen carrying submachine guns down Pennsylvania and Constitution avenues to the National Archives. Two days later, President Harry Truman declared at a formal ceremony in the Archives Exhibition Hall.

"We are engaged here today in a symbolic act. We are enshrining these documents for future ages. This magnificent hall has been constructed to exhibit them, and the vault beneath, that we have built to protect them, is as safe from destruction as anything that the wit of modern man can devise. All this is an honorable effort, based upon reverence for the great past, and our generation can take just pride in it."

Bibliographic note: *Web version based on the Introduction by Roger A. Bruns to A More Perfect Union: The Creation of the United States Constitution. Washington, DC: Published for the National Archives and Records Administration by the National Archives Trust Fund Board, 1986. 33 p.*

If Abraham's seeds want freedom, like the founding Europeans in America, you must understand how America achieved this. Look at the historical interest of freedom in America. It was declaration of independence, which they said, "*Give me Liberty or give me death*" and had less than twenty million people at that time. And God came among us and we are scared to death to declare our independence from our oppressor. We have to unite and request land and autonomy. God is present and we have knowledge of ourselves, so there should not be any fear of the devil. Some are afraid to speak this knowledge in front of the devil. But it is a new day now. Start getting the fear out of your hearts, and this is the time for re-educating and renewing our history. Knowledge is here, so there should be no fear or not knowing what is going on. Knowledge is all over Canada and England now, so America is showing stagnation to accept this knowledge. We must lift that banner of freedom, justice and equality and plant it within the shores and domains of North America. But you are taking this knowledge for granted. Psychologically, we must keep the lessons in mind so we can master all in the atmosphere. Thus, we are given a messenger, who was to make us all Allah. So, Allah is here as taught to us by "Pudding", the cream of the planet earth. Allah is but the Arabic name God.

Thus, the very constitution of America was for freedom and independence from England. I wanted to show that; since sharing mathematics as our common language and Islam as our way of living and we should organize and put forth a declaration of independence to the United States of America. Allah said: "**. . . in the fourth generation they shall come hither again: for the iniquity of the Amorites is not yet full**." [Gen. 15:16]. This means the devils will not give up so easy. He respects nothing, but his own filthy politics. He cares not about life and sees six, and the Bible states, ". . . Let him that hath understanding count the number of the beast: for it is the number of a man; and his number is six hundred threescore and six." [Rev. 13:18].

We represent "Him", who is Allah, the Supreme Being black man from Asia. God knows the time the devil has been on the planet earth. God is owner of earth and knowing devil; there would be no peace among them. So, they were placed on the worst part while we kept the warm parts. They lived in harsh-cold environment in the caves of Europe. Caucasians were making no history, until Musa. We are the seeds of Abraham. When Revelation said "Lion of the tribe of Judah, the Root of David" in the description of the Lamb, it could not be speaking of Muhammad who was white. It had to be no other than Elijah. The Ethiopian call themselves "Lion of the tribe of Judah", who are ancestors of David. J.A. Rogers' book can share some light on the real people of Abraham. Thus, when you deal with the *Lion of Judah* you are actually dealing with Ethiopia, and Muhammad of 1400 years ago knew that. So, this was not him. Ethiopia means "Burnt-face" in the Greek language to describe a people "black" and "comely". Comely is something or someone having attraction or attractive powers.

Amos 9:7

Are ye not as children of the Ethiopian unto me, O Children of Israel?

The Passover; a seven day celebration commemorating the exodus from Egypt. Christians calls this "Easter" and unaware of differences between the seventh day from the first day. It should be our festival. This was taken from us by those claiming genealogy to Abraham and are synagogue of Satan. Jose V. Malcioln's book states, "The history of Hebrews and Romans is easier to determine than the question of the chicken and the egg. With facts and dates, we do know how the Hebrews became Jews, and Romans became Italians." The African Origin of Modern Judaism, pg. 110. He continues, "After the Greeks learned religion and philosophy from Africa, they Hellenized it. The Greeks took Ethiopian gods like Ammon, worshipped at Ethiopia's ancient capital Meroe, and in Thebes, Egypt, and Libya. They called Ammon 'Zeus.' The Romans later called him 'Jupiter'." (Ibid, 110). So there is a science to all things. Seeds of Abraham must search history. We call this Asia, and devils it call Africa. Jose V. Malcioln's says, "The people whom the Hebrew called Cushites and the Greeks called Ethiopians were named by the former because they descended from Cush and the latter because of their beautiful skin color." ibid. p. 110. Mind you, Musa selected for himself an Ethiopian wife.

How did we look to Master Fard?

When Fard came he saw us as his people, who were lost from home, who had to be taught knowledge of self. He compared us to the Prodigal Son and Lazarus in the Bible. It appeared as though we were no people, just going around following teachings that do not fit us. Elijah taught us that Fard was around from the 1910-20, but made his appearance among us in 1930. He saw us as having no culture, yet knew that we were the original people of the planet. These are the seeds of Abraham that he was looking for. But they were so deep in the white man's alien culture that he called them "Uncle", meaning his father's brother. This was because he was a mixture of black and white. His father was a cold-knowledge seed (dark-skinned), and his mother was a Caucasians from the mountain. So, the Bible says, "**For what the law could not do, in that it was weak through the flesh, God sending his own Son in the likewise of sinful flesh, and for sin, condemned sin in the flesh**." [Romans 8:3].

He came to America by himself, yet did not go to the rich, who he named the ten percent (10%), and they were the rich slave-makers of the poor, who teaches the poor lies to believe that the almighty true and living God is a spook and cannot be seen by the physical eyes. Outside looking in, he saw us as being slaves from mental death and power, who were easily lead in the wrong directions, yet hard to be lead in the right directions. What the bible calls the "Lost Sheeps" he saw us as that and we had to be given knowledge of our origin in this world. Yeah, we were free, but we were not given knowledge of ourselves by the ones responsible for our bondage and emancipation. He looked for Elijah, for almost one year and in 1931 he found Elijah and it appeared that they both knew each other, since Elijah had the knowledge of the scripture already, so he knew God and had no problem knowing God when he ran into God. Elijah knew the bible, his father was a preacher. Thus, he made Elijah his Supreme Minister and taught him for three years. This can be related to the resurrection of Jesus as well. He went through three days and three nights through trials and tribulations under the enemy and the last day he came out and Jonah and Lazarus have the same signs. Fard taught all this to Elijah. He made sure that Elijah had the teaching down pack like a scientist, and it is a science which is the mathematical approach. He knew we did not speak our own language. However, there were two characteristics in the black man, one dominant and one recessive. This means some of us were house Negroes and others field Negroes. Some did love the devil and others hated the devil. But like the devil was brought out of our genes, he was in us. We can give birth to God or devil. Master Fard showed Elijah his mission by telling him all the secrets of his relationship to Elijah and the lost-found nation within the scriptures—Bible and Qur'an.

He gave Elijah his instructions, just as it was given to Moses and this was to separate the said people from their oppressors. Elijah was given the same duties. Elijah is the prophet like unto Moses. Fard taught Elijah that we were brought over here by the trader in the year fifteen-fifty, five (1555). Not only did he teach Elijah of his existence in the Bible, but he explain that our historical birth record do not exist, because we are the Alpha and Omega, the beginning that never began and the ending that will never end. He said he was prepared to come save us from the wicked, since we had been taken from our own biological roots for four hundred years. We have been lost from our own social equality, mis-educated and were taught to eat the wrong foods [swine and false teachings], and taught to fear the devil. He explained to Elijah that he is the One that the world has been waiting for, for the last 2,000 years. A "race" is what he taught Elijah that we were not, and that we are a nation. Negro or colored people were not proper to describe our population. How can Caucasians teach us our religion when he was given six-thousand years to rule us, until this One (Fard) comes to terminate the influence of the devil's education on our minds?

Master Fard said we do not belong to white people, and we belong to ourselves, free and independent. You beg the white man for everything. The lesson says, "That made him other than himself." Allah in the person of Pudding said we were "God of the universe". Although the NOI taught this but did not go in the Ghettoes of hell and teach the misguided youths in our community. The father taught the youths so much that Mayor Lindsay gave him the Allah school to continue his teaching. But this is the effect of the teachings of W.D. Fard. It produces Allah. Whoever learns from the lessons and understand them, they become very mathematical. Mathematics helps you think quickly and makes you swift and changeable. For Fard pointed out to Elijah that "My people are destroyed for the lack of knowledge . . ." [Hosea 4:6]. The number also shows you the signs of the numbers "4" and "6". Four hundred years (400) from the six thousand years (6,000). This is the year in the Asiatic Calendar Fifteen thousand (15,000), which is actually the year 1914, which was the expiration date of the devil's civilization. But now he threatens the righteous of being terrorist to put fear in your heart from accepting knowledge of yourself. He does not want us to know how filthy he is in all his affairs. He keeps us blind to ourselves so he can master us. When we start fighting and killing each other you know that there are devils among us. We just have to go to the fourth lesson in:

<u>Lost Found Muslim Lesson</u> #1 (1-14):

4. Why did we run Yacub and his made devil from the root of civilization over the hot Arabian Desert into the caves of West Asia as they now call it Europe? What is the meaning of Eu and Rope? How long ago? What did the devil bring with him? What kind of life did they live then? And how long before Musa came to teach them of their forgotten trick knowledge?

Ans. Because they started making trouble among the righteous people, accusing the righteous people of telling lies; causing them to fight and kill one another. Yacub was an original man and was the father of the devil. He taught the devil to do this devilishment. The root of civilization is in Arabia at the Holy City of Mecca, which means where the knowledge and wisdom of the original man started when the planet was first founded. We ran the devil over the hot Arabian Desert. We took from them everything except their language and made them walk every step of the way. It was two thousand-two-hundred miles. They went savage and lived in the caves of Europe. Eu means hillsides and Rope is the rope to bind in. It was 6,019 years ago. Musa came 2,000 years later and taught them how to live a respectful life, how to build a home for themselves and some forgotten trick knowledge that Yacub taught them which was devilishment - telling lies, stealing and how to master the original man. Musa was a half-original man and a prophet who was predicted by the 23 scientists in the year 1. 15,019 years ago from the date of this writing.

Thus, do not think that we were given these lessons and not watched by the devil's CIA agents, but Allah taught us to be fearless. We should deal with courage, which is the mastery of fear. The truth is here, there's no point in being fearful of the devil. When Malcolm X was taught in prison, he said that his educator was not fearful to speak his mind in front of the guards. Whatever truth he spoke was in front of anyone who witness this truth and this is where Malcolm X, El Hajj Malik Shabbazz learned to speak his mind. For when you are taught mathematics you have wings. There's a certain respect that you acquire and you begin to have the desire to increase your knowledge. Knowledge of yourself makes one fearless, and W.D. Fard had to get the fear out of our hearts so we can stand on our own perpendicular and in a square. He had to liberate us from the way the Caucasian power structure had us in mental bondage. Breaking that cycle of existence was taught to the messenger. Fard is said to be the educator of Noble Drew Ali, Marcus Garvey, Father Divine and Herbert Armstrong from the Plain Truth magazine. But his main student was Elijah. Elijah tells us that there were many jealous bodies as to him being the Messenger of Allah. They even tried to claim Elijah Muhammad's position. But Elijah is written in the book by name.

Fard even taught that his uncle would not know that he is their nephew. Why? Because they think Fard is white. Even if he was white he is our benefactor and we in the Nation of Gods and earths do not look at color if a man speaks the truth. Truth is truth regardless whose mouth it may come out of. Many people try to argue that W.D. Fard was Caucasian, when he had a black father. If he had a black father, then you know that three fifths of black man's blood you are black. Even besides that, everyone has our blood, because they come from us.

Acts 17:26

And hath made of **'One blood"** *all nations of men to dwell on all the face of the earth, and hath determined the times before appointed, and the bounds of their habitation.*

The Bible even shows that he comes in sinful flesh to condemn sin in the flesh. The Bible explains his existence. There is no way to discredit the history of Master Fard. It is written, and he knew that there would be those who disbelieve in the truth he put in the mouth of his student. "And it shall come to pass, that whosoever will not hearken unto my words which he shall speak in my name, which I will require it of him." [Deuteronomy 18:19]. Also in 18:15 tell you to listen to the messenger. Not only that but the Bible did not say he is "sinful flesh", but "likewise", meaning "looking like", since the name "Fard" means "disguise". So, he was the Son of man. The Bible says, "The Son of man is Lord even of the Sabbath day." (Matthew 12:8).

The entire Matthew chapter 24 is dealing with the coming of Fard and this is why Elijah knew who he was as soon as he made contact with Fard and, they were from opposite side of the world. Fard was from the east and Elijah was in the West, which was 9,000 miles away (32°: 1-36 English C lesson, #1). Since we could not swim that far physically and we did not have the knowledge of navigating the sea, after we were brought and indoctrinated by the alien-culture (the DEVIL). So, the Son of man had to come from the east. Let us see what Jesus had to say about the Son of man. His disciples asked him, "***Tell us, when shall these things be? And the end of the world?"*** (Matthew 24:30). Jesus answered and said unto them:

4 Take heed that no man deceive you.

5 For many shall come in my name, saying, I am Christ; and shall deceive many.

6 And ye shall hear of wars and rumours of wars: see that ye be not troubled: for all these things must come to pass, but the end is not yet.

7 For nation shall rise against nation, and kingdom against kingdom: and there shall be famines, and pestilences, and earthquakes, in divers places.

8 All these are the beginning of sorrows.

9 Then shall they deliver you up to be afflicted, and shall kill you: and ye shall be hated of all nations for my name's sake.

10 And then shall many be offended, and shall betray one another, and shall hate one another.

11 And many false prophets shall rise, and shall deceive many.

12 And because iniquity shall abound, the love of many shall wax cold.

13 But he that shall endure unto the end, the same shall be saved.

14 And this gospel of the kingdom shall be preached in all the world for a witness unto all nations; and then shall the end come.

15 When ye therefore shall see the **abomination of desolation**, spoken of **by Daniel** the prophet, stand in the holy place, (whoso readeth, let him understand:)

16 Then let them which be in Judaea flee into the mountains:

17 Let him which is on the housetop not come down to take any thing out of his house:

18 Neither let him which is in the field return back to take his clothes.

19 And woe unto them that are with child, and to them that give suck in those days!

20 But pray ye that your flight be not in the winter, neither on the sabbath day:

21 For then shall be great tribulation, such as was not since the beginning of the world to this time, no, nor ever shall be.

22 And except those days should be shortened, there should no flesh be saved: but for the elect's sake those days shall be shortened.

23 Then if any man shall say unto you, Lo, here is Christ, or there; believe it not.

24 For there shall arise false Christs, and false prophets, and shall shew great signs and wonders; insomuch that, if it were possible, they shall deceive the very elect.

25 Behold, I have told you before.

26 Wherefore if they shall say unto you, Behold, he is in the desert; go not forth: behold, he is in the secret chambers; believe it not.

27 *For as* **the lightning *cometh*** out of the east***, and*** *shineth* ***even*** *unto the west;* ***so shall also the coming of the Son of man be.***

28 For wheresoever the carcase is, there will the eagles be gathered together.

29 Immediately after the tribulation of those days shall the **sun** be darkened, and the **moon** shall not give her light, and the **stars** shall fall from heaven, and the powers of the heavens shall be shaken:

30 And then shall appear the sign of the Son of man in heaven: and then shall all the tribes of the earth mourn, and they shall see the Son of man coming in the clouds of heaven with power and great glory.

31 And he shall send his angels with a great sound of a trumpet, and they shall gather together his elect from the four winds, from one end of heaven to the other.

32 Now learn a parable of the fig tree; When his branch is yet tender, and putteth forth leaves, ye know that summer is nigh:

33 **So likewise ye, when ye shall see all these things, know that it is near, even at the doors**.

34 Verily I say unto you, This generation shall not pass, till all these things be fulfilled.

35 Heaven and earth shall pass away, but my words shall not pass away.

36 But of that day and hour knoweth no man, no, not the angels of heaven, but my Father only.

37 ***But as the days of Noah were, so shall also the coming of the Son of man be***.

38 *For as in the days that were before the flood they were eating and drinking, marrying and giving in marriage,* ***until the day that Noe entered into the ark,***

39 ***And knew not until the flood came, and took them all away; so shall also the coming of the Son of man be***.

40 Then shall two be in the field; the one shall be taken, and the other left.

41 Two women shall be grinding at the mill; the one shall be taken, and the other left.

42 **Watch therefore: for ye know not what hour your Lord doth come**.

43 But know this, that if the goodman of the house had known in what watch the thief would come, he would have watched, and would not have suffered his house to be broken up.

44 Therefore be ye also ready: for in such an hour as ye think not the Son of man cometh.

45 Who then is a faithful and wise servant, whom his lord hath made ruler over his household, to give them meat in due season?

46 Blessed is that servant, whom his lord when he cometh shall find so doing.

47 Verily I say unto you, That he shall make him ruler over all his goods.

48 But and if that evil servant shall say in his heart, My lord delayeth his coming;

49 And shall begin to smite his fellowservants, and to eat and drink with the drunken;

50 The lord of that servant shall come in a day when he looketh not for him, and in an hour that he is not aware of,

51 And shall cut him asunder, and appoint him his portion with the hypocrites: there shall be weeping and gnashing of teeth.

Allah came already in the person of W.D. Fard, in the person of Malcolm X's brother and then in the person of Clarence 13X, and we are the presence of God now in the person of the original man. They said the Son of man was killed and rose on the third day, and this is speaking about the black man, who W.D. Fard taught us to be. If we are to be him, then we are the Son of man, and this is why Allah in the person of Pudding took the name Allah for himself, since he had a more advanced understanding of who the original man was and lived it out without any religious doctrine, but understood the nature of such, but chose to shy away from these ritual. We did not recognize the five Pillars of Islam; except for signs that dealt with our origin in this world. After the Son of man was killed mentally for three (300) years, on the fourth he was resurrected by the Son of man, who taught the original man was God. So, he was resurrected back to his original self by the Messenger and disciple of Allah in the person of Master Fard. God always reveals the secrets and mysteries to his disciples and servants. ***And that servant, which knew his lord's will, and prepared not himself, neither did according to his will, shall be beaten with many stripes***. (Luke 12:47). Our duty is to teach the babies and build our own social equality, our own economic structure and build our own individual power. We need land, real estate, hospitals and schools. This is what the blue print of God is and we were given knowledge and not only wisdom, but understanding of all things in existence. The lesson says, "The nation of Islam is all-wise and does everything right and exact", so we are God of the universe. It's our fourth-hundredth year in the Wilderness as Ezekiel describe us as dried bones, we shall be given light--to mentally be given life. We were only mentally dead. In all the history of Islam the dead is never known to return from the grave.

In the "thirtieth" year, "a whirlwind came out of the north" which brought brightness that was an expansion in any man or woman's mind. Marcus Garvey said he would come back as a "whirlwind", could it be that Marcus Garvey Had this knowledge of Fard as well? For Elijah said the appearance of Fard was like a flash of light in a very dark place. Jesus says the way you can tell who the Son of man is, would be by his origin and destiny, [Matt. 24:23], "Then if any man shall say unto you, Lo, here is Christ, or there; believe it not."

For there shall *arise false Christs*, and *false prophets*, and shall shew great signs and wonders; insomuch that, if it were possible, they shall deceive the very elect . . .Behold, I have told you before . . .Wherefore if they shall say unto you, Behold, he is in the desert; go not forth: behold, he is in the secret chambers; believe it not . . . *For as the lightning cometh out of the east, and shineth even unto the west; so shall also the coming of the Son of man be.*

Jesus never travelled from east to the west (here). Neither did Muhammad. They never travelled more than 9,000 miles in their lifetime. Thus, the Son of man could not be a title for Jesus, since he was supposed to have no human father according to Christians and orthodox Muslims, unless you agree with the concept of man being God. However, this title is dealing with Master Fard. Just as the Christians claim that they are followers of Jesus, but you have to question this. Are you followers of Jesus? Are you the children of Israel? This is who he taught. Jesus even says: ". . . ***In vain they do worship me***, teaching for ***doctrines*** the ***commandments of men***." He makes known this is not Allah's mathematics to worship him or any other man. You can respect a man, but not worship them as the only God; this is why Allah in the person of Pudding said to let no one deny you of being Allah, even if the world denied you. Whatever they were, we are now and they wanted us to be better, because THERE are no limits to what one can do. This entire blueprint was right in our DNA, before we caused the electron, neutron and protons to give off sparks of burning gases as a compound called "Atom", which is **A**llah **t**he **O**riginal **M**an. Also this brought forth the great luminary known as the sun, which keeps burning the helium and hydrogen. So we are Alpha and Omega, since we are the original, pre-Adamites, proto-type; and the primal origin of all people in the universe. If white people were the original people on the earth, the earth would only be one kind of people and that is white. They can only produce their own kind. So, we have a blueprint to take our planet back from the devil. We do not want to put a black devil for a white one. A devil is a devil. A wise righteous man will rule with truth and justice.

Thus, when you plan, study and develop new ways of doing things, with the guidance of your foundation (120°), then and only then you becoming a builder and master of the Day of Judgement. These are the days of Allah, and this is Allah's Word Manifested. Having knowledge is not just to talk about it, but building wealth, and having an economic blueprint. If one of the Gods or earths comes home, there should be businesses where we can offer those jobs. If you are not thinking like that, then we are a lost nation and we will continue to be in the bottom of the ladder of civilization. Yet, those who are thinking in terms of wealth, you are in the right track. I don't care how many degrees you can quote. After all of this you are still subject to a people who know mathematics. Those with mathematics build and do not spend idle time talking about what's going on, but make things happen themselves. When you have mathematics you build your own social equality. How do you do that? You know social means to advocate a society of men or group of men for one common cause? Equality means to be equal in everything. Otherwise, this does not mean we are socialist or communist, or dealing with capitalistic persuasions, but we deal with what is right and beneficial to us as a nation. Well, I will prove that Allah can come in the person of a man, and I will use:

Concept of Incarnation and Vishnu's Ten Avataras

Article of the Month - July 2009

The concept of 'avatar' - incarnation, is the foremost cardinal of Hinduism. An incarnation - descent of God in whatever form He chose to emerge on the earth for accomplishing a divine objective, or presenting an absolute model of life or sublimating a virtue, along with accomplishing such divine objective, is considered in Hindu way of life a cosmic reality occurring from time to time or when it became emergent for re-setting the world to order.

The Muslims other than NOI thinks that God never came in the form of a man, but here's the concept of 'avatar' stating that God can be manifested in whatever form he chose to show and prove his existence. This is why I say you can give birth to God or devil, and this is why you have two germs in you black man- a positive and a negative [a dominant- a recessive]. Now you have the purpose of applying these mathematical equations to fulfill a certain function and purpose, which is to establish your own social equality. We have to build a society that is God conscious and centered, which is a theocracy, but we do everything right and exact. You want a better world, so you have to have God remove all the negativities in you and accept the will of God, who is the Supreme Being, black man from Asia. Otherwise, the Asiatic Black man, the maker, the owner, the cream of the planet earth, father of civilization and God of the universe. So now you may be wondering why God made devil. For Let us follow that in the next chapter.

Then why did God make devil?

The answer to that question was answered by Elijah in the said response:

To show forth his power, that he is all wise and righteous, that he could make a devil, which is weak and wicked and give him the power to rule for 6,000 years, then destroy him in one day without falling a victim to the devil's civilization. Otherwise to show and prove that Allah is God, always has been and always will be.

This lesson is letting you know that the devil is in you and that he was taken out of you and given form and shape. If the devil was not in you, he would have never been brought forth. If you are an original man, then you do not have to worry about coming after something else, but being the aborigines of the planet. "Ab" is from a Greek root word meaning "From" and "Origines" means "beginning". We are the people from the beginning. A scientist realized that 6,698 years ago! Yacub was the father of the Caucasians. He was the God that ruled for 6,000 years, who taught them devilishment: Telling lies, stealing and how to master the original man. The original man consists of black, brown and yellow. The body (5% NGE) says we have sixteen shades of brown and 16 shades of yellow. Thus, after the pattern and blood of the original man Yacub discovered that in the black is a brown man and in the brown man a yellow man and in the yellow man a white man. After following 600 years of dealing with a mild form of birth control law he was able to eliminate the black into a brown and come with the yellow. In the 600th year he had a Caucasian type people who were all recessive traits. So, what he did was use a dominant trait to beget a recessive trait. Suppose the black man produce four-hundred million albinos? Are you saying that it is impossible? This is proof that we are father of all human beings.

Yacub saw this before Caucasians were even on the earth physically. He brought the devil out from within us. This is why the bible tells you:

And God said, Let us make man in our image, after our likeness: and let them have dominion over the fish of the sea, and over the fowl of the air, and over the cattle, and over all the earth, and over every creeping thing that creepeth upon the earth.

Genesis 1:26

God is saying, "Let us" what? "Make a man" How? "In our image" How? "After our likeness", not the original, but has likeness of the first one, after our proto-type. We know he won't look exactly like the original, but he will be leprous, white as snow, as a form of punishment for being born in sin, since the nature in which he was born was of telling lies, stealing and not honoring the Father and mother of all human beings, who is God and his black woman (earth). He will be colored, because when you color something you alter it, and this man's nature is colored, because he is here to change civilization. He is here to "have dominion" over the earth. Not to omit the scientist who made them, gave this man special instructions:

Be fruitful, and multiply, and replenish the earth, and subdue it: and have dominion. (Gen. 1:28)

You be fruitful and multiply, because you have to increase your population, and when you do that; you replace (replenish) the original rulers (Black man) after I place you on the earth.

[HQ. 2:31] And God said: 'I am about to place a vicegerent in the earth,' they said: 'Wilt Thou place therein such as will cause disorder in it, and shed blood?' He answered: 'I know what you know not.'

Thus, he made Caucasians to check us into seeing what was in you and to master it with a more re-collective and omnipotent mind. If you know that is what came out of you, then you know to keep it out of you so you do not follow the children of Adam. We are pre-Adamites, who the Adamites were made in the likeness of. So, the devil was made to show and prove that Allah is God, always has been and always will be. Also to show forth and prove that he is all wise and righteous, that he can make a devil that is weak and wicked, give him the power to rule for 6,000 years, then destroy him in one day without falling a victim to the devil's civilization.

Now, if the devil was to rule with his colored regulations for 6,000 years, then we were living according to his rules and regulations. This is why we have to fight for our rights, since his laws were not for us. He did not view others as he wrote his laws. He does not like the original people, who are black, brown and yellow. They all have a little Hitler in them, so says Khalid Muhammad on the Phil Donahue show. And that is true. You can always detect their frustrations when they come in that form. Elijah says "Some snakes are more harmful than others", but they are still snakes. But they hate everyone non-white and Malcolm X said, "No one knows the master better than the slave"; and that is also correct, especially if he has been given knowledge of himself. You can tell by the mind that the devils displays and when you tell him about himself, he is afraid and accuse you of being hateful, when actually he is the hateful one. Any white society you go to you will see that there is white racist and supremacy there and there is no denying this. America is the leader of the world. This is the land that we have no justice from the white power structure. We are shot, imprisoned and treated so harshly under the government of the Europeans. Obama is president and you see outright disrespects towards his presidency. You can feel the hate stimulated by the whites. His nature is different from the original people. But somehow they are now trying to be us and do what we do, because he was made to try to make a mockery out of us and steal our culture at the same time and you are not even aware of this. So, this is a colored people (mankind). He is a kind of man.

Albino is a person with pale skin, light hair, pinkish eyes, and visual abnormalities resulting from a hereditary inability to produce the pigment melanin. Do white people produce melanin? They produce less than three fifth of melanin. They are recessive traits. Thus, Caucasians are an abnormality and genetic deficiency. They are actually albinos. So when a black man produces an albino it actually shows that he is genetically capable of producing the human family. Just like the Bible tells us in Act 17:26, on page 40, where that ***one blood*** is the black man's one. If this was the Caucasian man's blood, we would only have one type of people in the world, since they only have the capacity to beget only recessive traits. Two whites cannot produce any other than their own type and kind. Once they have a non-white mate, the baby is non-white. However, if you mix with black, the baby can come out like W.D. Fard, J.A. Rogers and W.E. B. Dubois, or they can come out like Barack Hussein Obama, Halle Berry or Bob Marley.

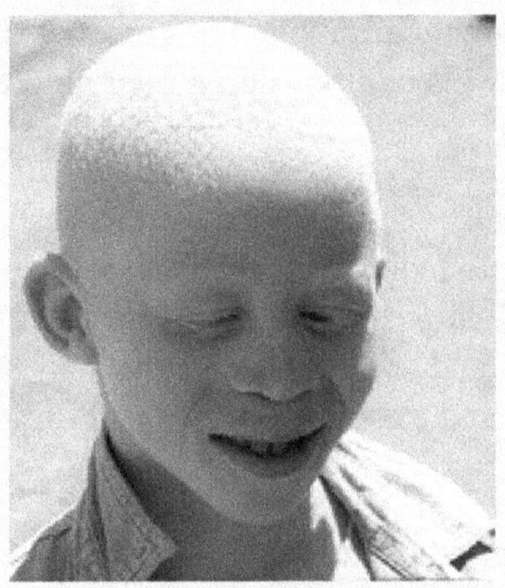

This is an albino youth.

It is noted by the Tanzania Albino Society (TAS) has registered 8,000 of the 150,000 albinos there, and they are a target for murder and other atrocities in Tanzania, by witch doctors and things of that nature. And that is probably the same thing that happened when white people first got into contact with black people, after they were grafted on the island of Patmos, also known as Pelan. The black man would murder them and run them from among us for looking so strange and unalike. Not every black man would murder them but the ones that dealt with witchcraft. They thought that certain parts of their bodies would bring success to society or magical powers for good luck. Tanzania is thought to be the highest population of the albinos in Africa, in which we call it Asia. That is dealing with the seventh lesson in the Lost-Found Muslim lesson #1 (1-14). "Why does the devil call our people Africans?" However, here is an article by Noah:

NOAH - The National Organization for Albinism and Hypopigmentation

African-Americans with Albinism

Many people ask if the incidence of albinism in non-whites is higher than in whites. The answer is no. The incidence seems higher because people with albinism born into non-white races are more instantly recognizable, and because traditional studies of albinism have been done in smaller closely related tribes where there seem to be more affected individuals. [They are albinos] Emphasis mines.

Physical Differences

Whereas the majority of whites with albinism have pale blond or white hair, pink white skin, and blue eyes, black persons with albinism tend to have hair of a deeper, brighter yellow, cream-colored skin, and green or hazel eyes.

Although the physical problems of low vision and sun sensitivity are the same for both whites and non-whites, the social problems of non-whites are compounded. In the Caucasian races blond hair, blue eyes, and alabaster skin are considered so highly desirable that brunettes often bleach their hair or wear colored contacts. The Victorians wore white wigs and powdered their skin to a chalky white. Fairy tale heroines are said to have skin white as snow.

The same physical attributes in darker races are taboo. Individuals in these races often are ostracized because of erroneous beliefs and unfounded fears. A basic theme in many variations in that God is delivering judgment on a family with albinism and that the individual with albinism is cursed, or is the embodiment of sin. In some religions and societies, this curse may seem true. Anyone taking as a partner a person with albinism must be prepared to suffer ridicule and disapproval from family, friends, or even the church.

Another belief is that the person with albinism is the result of incest or inbreeding. The most common myth of today is that the non-Caucasian person with albinism must be the result of mixed marriage. Those who hold this view are unaware that people with albinism existed in societies of color before those societies had any contact with Caucasians.

Peers sometimes accuse black people with albinism of "trying to pass." Indeed, some have found having albinism so painful that it is simply easier to be "white." Peers may believe that the hard-earned achievements of a black person with albinism resulted from a white teacher or supervisor favoring the him or her.

The Family of Color with Albinism Misunderstanding of the causes of albinism is sometimes the catalyst for extra family stress. An already distrusting and jealous father may feel that his partner has cheated on him with a white man. He may be unable to accept the child as his. He may treat mother and child harshly, or even leave altogether, goaded by family and friends. Though the mother knows that she has been faithful, only recently has blood testing allowed her to prove it. If the father stays, he may make the child with albinism the target of subtle or outright resentment. Family dysfunction such as alcoholism, drug abuse, or mental illness may compound the problems for the child.

If the mother feels "stuck" with childcare and custody, she may abuse or even abandon the child. She may endure disapproval from both races, because some people still frown upon what they assume to be interracial coupling. Mothers have reported being mistaken for baby-sitters, or in extreme cases, kidnappers.

On the other hand, many parents, after their initial shock, say they feel that their albino child is a special gift to them. They find the "golden" children attractive and welcome additions to the family, and they are quite proud of them.

School age children and teenagers with albinism often find themselves left out of extracurricular activities and social events by other black youth. Children with albinism may learn to avoid rejection by withdrawing. The child's peers then may see him or her as unfriendly or even hostile, and a cycle of isolation is set up.

Children with albinism may learn to compensate for their lack of self-esteem by striving harder in school and other activities. They tend to exceed at whatever they try. Many Black people with albinism have succeeded as technicians, legal assistants, entrepreneurs, computer programmers, preachers, college professors . . . the list goes on and on. Once overcoming the low self-esteem brought on by early social stigma, people with albinism often become high achievers.

Coping

Coping and dealing with albinism has run the gamut from being militant in one's racial conviction to wearing dark make-up and hair color or surgically altering one's appearance to pass for white. Some may argue that these may not be coping at all. From my point of view, coping meant coming to the realization that this is exactly what the creator wanted me to be. My albinism was present with me since my creation, from the earliest stages of development in the uterus. I am a typical person with albinism. My hair, skin, and eye color are in no way different from other non-white people with albinism. To me, albinism is a situation no different than that of a redhead being born into a family of brunettes.

My other coping mechanism is the realization that albinism is an old, old "race." We have been recorded in every part of the world, in every era, in every culture known to humans. It has been said that we may represent in fact the oldest recorded genetic condition.

Virginia Small, NOAH Director Reviewed by the NOAH Albinism Awareness Committee: James Haefemeyer, MD, MS, Chair, NOAH Board of Scientific Advisors; Janice Knuth, MSW, ACSW, LSW, President, NOAH 1982-1993; Charla McMillan, MS, President, NOAH, 1996-2000; Michael McGowan, President, NOAH, 2001-2002.

Actually they are letting you know that albinos were here before Caucasians. They are not saying it like that, but you can tell if you know the science of Yacub or the teachings of Frances Cress Welsing. You can tell that it don't take white people for black man to produce albinos. When it says that black man does not trust the relationship, when he has an albino baby on top of it he believes that his woman has cheated on him. However, God do not speak like that. You do not hear the Gods talking about cheated on so, and cheated on whom. That's not a part of our vocabulary. So, albinos were used to bring forth Caucasians and it would not take 600 years to produce them, but if you used all albinos like Yacub did on an island, in two hundred years or less you would have at least seventeen million Caucasians. We were in America for a little over four-hundred years and it's about 30 to 40 million of us now. In learning and understanding the lessons, Bible or Qur'an you must have vision and observation and you can see what was yesterday is now today. The Bible says it like this, "But as the days of Noah were, so shall also the coming of the Son of man be." [Matthew 24:37].

When living in the days of Noah, there was a flood destroying all those who were outside what he called the ark, and saved those who had knowledge of God and accepted the teachings of Noah. All that were not in agreement with the truth in which Noah spoke were destroyed and so shall it be in the "last Days" in which the Son of man will come. He calls his messenger to get you off the drugs, alcohol and the negativity. The messenger made the call for you to do for self and get away from the devil's alien-culture. You actually see people on top of their house and on boats trying to get away from the storms and hurricane and earthquakes. Hurricane Sandy came right on Halloween October 31, 2012, because Allah is fed up with the devil. Recently there was a meteor that was shot on the earth. "The Russian meteor -- estimated to be just 10 tons and about 15 meters or 49 feet wide -- entered the Earth's atmosphere at a hypersonic speed of at least 33,000 mph and shattered about 18-32 miles above the ground. It released the energy of several kilotons above the Chelyabinsk region." - Andrew Cheng of the Johns Hopkins Applied Physics Laboratory.

All above is caused by the Son of Man. Wherefore, Jesus said to his disciples, "Tell the vision to no man, until the Son of man be risen again from the dead." (Matt.17:9). We are the Son of man and are risen from a mental dead stage so we can now tell the vision because Elijah came, Allah who came after Elijah and we are here to represent him. We can express this truth to infinity. Allah is God and he did not teach us to worship him. He even said he was our older brother. He did not want for us to worship him. He said we should be better than him.

Thus, the meteorite hit Russia on 15th of February 2013; which is part of the house of Gog and Magog. In the south is the Caucasus Mountain. And this was the same place that the Caucasian man inhabited when they were ran into the Caucasus Mountain, in what they call west Asia. Georgia is right within the

Caucasus Mountain. On December 7, 1988 there was an earthquake of 7.0 on the Richter scale on the Caucasus Mountain, within Armenia and 60,000 people died, which is the same number of people that Yacub took to the island of Patmos, an island situated by the Agean Sea. He took 59,999 and with himself made 60,000. Earthquakes are caused by the Son of man experimenting with high explosive. Now that we know who God and devil are we must build according to that. But those Caucasians, who can be righteous, try to go against the nature that you were made. Study and be good to the human family and be independent of the other devils. Yet, although the lessons say you are devils, but we do not judge you according to that, like you judge us according to our skin, yet we respect all people. Also after 600 years, the Pope has stepped down, which shows the sign of the devil being made and taken down, with his number. It is a number of a man "*six, threescore and six*". Six hundred years, but what happened to the other sixty-six? Sixty-six is the Sixty-six trillion years ago deportation of the moon from the earth, according to Elijah Muhammad. But like I said he was made by six hundred years of grafting and separating of birth control law, had power to rule for six thousand years, and has six ounces of brains. He is a six-million- Dollar man.

After self-knowledge, then what?

After the knowledge of self we are supposed to build and destroy, build the positive and destroy the negative. You must do first things first. When you build up, you actually must break down that which is a burden to you. A builder will eliminate stumblingblock in his everyday existence and take care of things that matters most to him first. We call this the foundation. A ruler must rule his kingdom in proper order. If a civilize person does not perform his duty, he will fall by his own iniquity. Anything by nature that you neglect, it will slowly disappear. As a plant, if you do not take proper care of a plant, it will not grow into a fruitful tree. However, if you give the plant all the necessary ingredients and nutrients it needs to grow into a tree, then it's on its way to be fruitful. The plant will bear fruit and that is just the Laws of nature. When you do not take care of yourself, people can see that. They know that you are not clean through your actions and ways. But if you are clean people detect this. It's easy to detect your type, whether you are clean or dirty. A tree bears the fruit of its kind and type. Thus, if you have a problem, then you must work on that problem until you have the potential and power to solve the problem. Any problem can be solved, so long you have willingness to recognize that problem and fix it. This is using the knowledge that you have. This is why Jesus says, "The truth shall set you free". That is right and exact.

If you know the existence of something, then you know the history of that thing. If you know the distance of your destination, and know how long it takes to get there and you have to get there at certain time, then automatically you calculate all the things that will hold you back and master that and make way to overcome that and get there on time. You have to have wisdom, which is good judgment. Having good judgment is being in tune with mathematics and this applies to everything in life. You can tell what is real and what isn't. If someone tells you that a plane parked in your closet, you know the size of your closet and the size of the plane, and automatically know that is impossible. And this is how your culture should be. Islam is what we call mathematics and is the natural and actual facts. When dealing with mathematics it is a product of the Son of man, not a product of something mysterious or spooky. And we as black people gave this to the world. Yet this is what we were given the lessons for, to be swift and changeable according to the situation. And this is why the father said we are not pro-black or anti-white. This is true, because if the situation is not called for being pro-black, then we are not in support of it. Yet, if the white are doing something good for the community we are not necessarily anti-white. Depending on the situation we become pro-righteous and anti-devilishment. If we take out a devil, we do not want to replace the devil with a black one. We do not want devils. Knowing this you have to approach everything as a master. After a hard times and going through trials and tribulations you know that you went through it and came out victorious. This is the concept of mathematics. Mathematics is living energy, the essence of all motions, forces, the revolution of the planets, which is activity or life.

So, with knowledge of self, never spend too much idle times doing nothing. Spend time mastering yourself and your universe, regardless to whom or what. Study and read books that inspires you and listens to music to embed the thoughts in your heart and mind. This is all good. Play songs that are positive that nurture your thoughts and feelings and you half-way there. In fact, you are there. Just do what makes you happy as long as it brings beneficial result to your cipher. You do not want to abuse substance and think that is good for you. Control that. That is a problem. Your duty is to bring forth beneficial results. You build what your community needs: A super market, schools, hospitals, food, clothing and real-estates. We have to think bigger than just talking. Some say, "Yeah, you talk that talk, but don't walk the walk." But although, we should not worry about other's words about us, but people can see, just like I said in the first paragraph of this chapter, a tree bears the fruit of its type. You want to be a doctor; start reading the book of medicine, a lawyer read the book of law, or a scientist the book of science. Keep yourself busy. You have to set goals for yourself and test yourself to see if you can reach them, and do that regardless to whom or what, and at any given time at any given place. This could be applied with self, family, a nation or an army. Even if you want to be a meteorologist, we have the knowledge of what causes rain, hail, snow and earthquakes. We would have to study to show ourselves approved. "And that servant, which knew his lord's will, and prepared not himself, neither did according to his will, shall be beaten with many stripes." [Luke 12:47]. You will be beaten with the stripes of failure, disrespects and being labeled an uneducated looser. First, know yourself and then learn all in your universe and learn how to navigate throughout the atmosphere, and you have to be the supreme navigator. You do not have to be in the ocean to navigate. And the father taught us in that manner.

Clarence 13X knew that the Blackman was God. So, he called himself Allah. Justice C. Allah, known as "Old Man Justice", a.k.a. Free Cipher Akbar, Abu Shahid formerly known as John 37X, and Ebeca were his disciples, that we call the "first borns". Allah guided nine young brothers from Mecca (Harlem), aged from thirteen to twenty-two. Allah was called "The Father" by his disciples because they came from broken homes and he became father figure in their lives, and they thought he was strong. Most people who tried to teach the young were unsuccessful, but Allah came with such dynamic wisdom that they knew he was no joke. So, they quickly accepted Pudding as their mathematical father and he gave them ***The Supreme Mathematics*** and The ***Supreme Alphabets***. Mathematics was taken from ***Supreme Wisdom***, which became ***120 lessons***. Thus, it is taught by some elders that Abu Shahid was partner in putting the Supreme Mathematics and Alphabets together. Elijah always said after him Allah will come, so he was the one who fulfilled that position and Elijah did not disagree with him. I remember that I read a plus degree that the two met and Elijah said so "It's you". But Allah had no problems with FOI or with Elijah's NOI. He left on his own. But he was not going to throw away the foundation of his seeds, the seeds of Abraham. And for those agents who want to disagree, do that, but if you are for real about the state of the nation of Gods and earth you will teach the truth. However, the teaching of God as a man is older than the sun, moon and stars, whether they know it or not. We must master all ciphers. All this was in the beginning. "And the sons of God saw the daughters of men." So, you have the sons of God and you have the sons of the devil. By sons, they are speaking on the right hand of those close to either one—God or devil. Both are man.

October 10, 1964 is our announcement as the Nation of the 5% of Gods and earths. And we have been influencing all types of culture and styles since then. We have given new vocabulary to the black community, which reaches the whole earth. We gave birth to hip hop by having ciphers and quoting our 120 lessons and inspired Cool Herc, known as Clive Campbell, born to Nettie Campbell and Keith Campbell in Kingston, Jamaica in 1966. So, he was only a youth when the Gods started to have ciphers and go to parties and stand on the square, which was the right arm folded over the left, and they called that the B-boy stand by others, but known to the 5% as the square. He came to the United States in 1967, same year Sham God designed our flag, the first ***nine borns*** was gaining grounds in all five boroughs and in 1969, the father returned to the essence of life, so the nation was running wild. The Malcolm X book described us as the "***Blood Brothers***", because they asked Malcolm X if they are his people and he said "Yes, they are my blood brothers." How can a man deny their brother? They had killed some white people and they were questioning Malcolm X and he told them that we were his brothers. But Cool Herc did not create hip hop, he just put it in an entrepreneurial perspective. He will tell you that he learned from other DJ's and showed his knowledge by sciencing it up (drawing up) all the things he needed to become the best and standing apart from the rest. But hip hop did not start at 1520 Sedgwick Towers, which was the housing authority in the Bronx, where Cool Herc lived. But he did start the musical science of it, with putting different break beats to it, but he just added on to what was already in effect. You know black man is God, whether he knows it or not and he can bring things into existence with nothing but his thoughts. So, this was a revolutionary time for black men then to be fruitful and multiply. It was an evolution of God's culture, but it was all ours. But you can see the God in Cool Herc if you read his history. Big up to all the DJs of today and those that knows me. Let us start with Clue, Rello and Jadel, Showtime (Jay Moe Ice), Chubby Chubb, Ike Love, Holliwood, Craig-g and all those I have not mentioned. Kay Slay is one I should not forget, he brought my last book. You all made history. Thus, we must continue to bring things in existence. Our teachings are very strong. And we must continue to elevate to the heights of perfection, which is infinity; for we are cream of the planet earth, father of civilization and God of the universe.

I remember God Allah, from the Desert told me that Africa Bambaataa used to be 5% and come to the rallies. He is known as the Amen Ra and "Godfather" of hip hop culture, but he got it from the Gods. The wisdom was attractive and they had to create a lifestyle to go with it through the music. Drop science on the mic and show and prove are two of the hip hop vocabulary that originated from the Gods. If you read the history of Bambaataa in the book by Jeff Chang, by the title, Can't Stop, Won't Stop: A History of the Hip-Hop Generation, you can see the influence of the Gods in the hip hop culture. George Nelson also wrote a book called Hip Hop America that drops little jewels in it for those who would like to know the existence of our influence on the hip hop ciphers.

Hip hop was not something made with all the gangster portrayal. It was based on taking young people out of the gangs and stopping the violence and this was the teachings of the Gods, to save the babies. And Bambaataa was the type to science out what was needed for the community babies. By babies I am speaking of those from 10 on up to 20 years of age. Thus, he had changed his gang (Black Spades) into the Universal Zulu Nation. There were Parties on the block, at the park; where they used power from the street lights for their equipments (DJ equipments) and rhyme with music playing. This is what rappers do today. The equipments consist of a mixer and the two turn-tables and the mic, which is the microphone. But now they are trying to take all that away, and coming up with ways to kill our culture, since this culture has influence the world. Thus, we have to take over the world and organize that power, just like Bambaataa organized his nation, but as a whole and on a bigger scale, under the banner of freedom, justice and equality. It's time that all black people be free and have our own society or social equality. We do not want to beg the devil for what we can get on our own. And this is our blueprint, from the almighty true and living God, from the beginning where knowledge and wisdom of the original man first started.

Although, Marcus Garvey did not teach that the black man is God, but he did say we had to see God through our own image and interest. But that is another way to say you are God. We never taught to go back to Africa, since we have contributed so much in America and so many gave their lives for us to be here. Thus, the lessons helped us to recognize all freedom fighters of the world. However, we do not disagree with those who want to go back to Africa. This is their choice and we respect all those who apply to the concept. But we are the future rulers of the world with this knowledge. We have to get politically strong as a people by getting involved. Not only that we are a nation, but if we want freedom, we have to say "Be" and it is. Allah comes in person and it is coming out in me right now. Like Jesus says, "I and my father are one". This goes back all the way to Osiris and the Pharaohs. But we gave America all of our culture and our inventions only to be hated and disrespected by their Caucasian hateful birds. Many inventions in America were by black people in America. Maulana Karenga in his book Introduction to Black Studies, pg. 160, says: "***Some of the most important inventions contributing to this industrialization process were by African Americans* (*Diggs*, *1975;* *Adams*, *1979;* *Carwell*, *1977;* *Hayden*, *1972;* *Haber*, *1970;* *Klein*, *1971*)." Not only that, but Karenga explains that not all the invention were recognized before the year 1861. ". . . Black inventions were hardly recognized or known due to the fact that enslaved Africans could not patent their inventions. In fact in 1858, the U.S. Attorney General ruled that since a slave was not a citizen and a patent was a contract between the government and a citizen inventor, a slave could not make a contract with the government or assign the invention to the slaveholder."

Thus, you see the colored man (Caucasians) robbed us every way they could. And even today, they look at us with contempt and all the sudden when you know the truth, they will accused the truth teacher of being the evil one, the one who preach hates. But we did not write your history, it was written by your hands in blood. Your record on the earth shows you causing confusion amongst the original people, accusing the people of telling lies, causing them to fight and kill one another. He puts mother against father, daughter against brother; parents against their children and family against family. But when one tells of his history he shies away and starts making accusations. He calls you "Un-American", "Homo-phobic" and all types of other names. When we learn about him we will run him from among us. But our Messenger was sent to us, "Remember ye the Law of Moses my servant, which I commanded unto him in Horeb for all Israel, with the statutes and judgments . . . Behold, I will send you Elijah the prophet before the coming of the great and dreadful day of the Lord. . . ***And he shall turn the heart of the fathers to the children, and the heart of the children to their fathers, lest I come and smite the earth with a curse.*** " [Malachi 4:4-6]

Thus, we must remember to prepare ourselves to become future rulers and have powers relocated to us. Obama was a sign for us as he became the 44th president of the United States, for the 4.4 billion black people all over the world. We have been in America for 458 years now. Look at the numbers of the above prophecy. Obama is chapter 4; verse 4 and you have 5 and 6. So the date is pretty accurate. He is just a start, but this is a sign that we will have the ultimate power soon. Meteorite is being shot from the heavens showing the Son of man's power is coming from the clouds of heavens into the earth, to show that our time is here just like the prediction. It is here and you see the Caucasians on boats, on top of their houses due to the storms happening in America to change the shift of power. You all must bow down to the original man and there won't be any peace if you do not bow down, and this is why Moses said to, "**Honour thy father and thy mother: that thy days may be long upon the land which the Lord thy God giveth thee**." [Exodus 20:12]. But the Bible says there will be storms and earthquakes, "And all the people saw the thunderings, and the lightnings, and the noise of the trumpet, and the mountain smoking: and when the people saw it, they removed, and stood afar off" [Ex. 20:18]. I remember that Richard Pryor was making jokes about meeting God in 1930 and he got all messed up afterwards and Eddie Murphy said, "I don't do God Jokes; you see what happened to Richard Pryor?" So, you know who Pryor was speaking upon? If he had taken heed to the one who came in the person of Fard, he would not have turned out like he did.

What about the Buddha's teachings?

Buddha is Allah, and you can see the teachings of the Buddha were the same as the 5% teachings, which is the transformation of self into a higher enlightenment by going through hell or suffering. Experiencing tribulations, utilizing your energy towards self-mastery and transforming your suffering into a state of happiness. The NGE calls this state in the Supreme Alphabets, twelfth (12th) degree LOVE, HELL or RIGHT. You have to go through hell to come out right or Victorious. Why did Musa have a hard time civilizing the devil in the year 2,000 B.C.? He had a hard time because the devil was extremely savage, but after the hard time the job was completed. So, everything you do in life will be tested. Buddha who was born Siddhartha Gautama, as a child, Siddhartha the Buddha, was troubled by some of the same thoughts that children today have. They wonder about birth and death. They wonder why they get sick and why grandfather died. They wonder why their wishes do not come true. Children also wonder about happiness and the beauty in nature. Because the Buddha knew what was in the hearts of children and human kind, he taught everyone how to live a happy and peaceful life. Buddhism is not learning about strange beliefs from faraway lands. It is about looking at and thinking about our own lives. It shows us how to understand ourselves and how to cope with our daily problems. And this was the purpose of our Supreme wisdom came into effect by W.D. Fard who transformed us into Allah, and we are thankful for all our representatives. Buddha is the same, since he came for the purpose.

Buddha, Gautama, was not the first Buddha, just as Fard and Clarence was not the first embodiment that manifested themselves as God, but there were Pharaohs who said they were God. In fact, J.A. Roger described the first images of the Ancient of Days, God, as black and having woolly haired. And so did Daniel in the Bible. And Buddha has such hair-type. One of the attributes of Buddha is "Krishna", meaning the "dark-one" or "black" in the Sanskrit language. But there was other Buddha before Gautama. He saw a monk who gave up everything one day to learn how to solve the problem of suffering and he learned from the monk, and at this point he learned from the Monk his mission and determined idea what his future would be. Everything is caused by the Son of man. All the great elders had to have something to stimulate the God within you. Just as Buddha, Muhammad Ali and Clarence Smith X, known as "Pudding" and the father of civilization, they were inspired to be or become through something that they came into contact with. And their eyes were opened for them to see it, with the third eye (the mind). Buddha had written lessons as well to show and prove himself as being Buddha (Allah). So, don't be confined to just 120° lessons, but try to solve all mysteries of the universe. We do not worship another man, since you have the equal power with any man that teaches in the universe. You can be lesser, equal or greater. But they all learned to give others the knowledge of how to maintain a clean and healthy living by applying some principles and obeying certain formulas for a successful existence.

Buddha was the "Enlighten" or "Awaken One", and this goes for all of us, since we do not deny truth after it has come to us, so he was called, Shakyamuni Buddha, just as the Clarence became "The father" and Elijah the "Messenger of Allah" and W.F. Muhammad or W.D. Fard, "The Son of Man". The key to their relationship is mathematics and the science of everything in life. This is why he came out with his own mathematics, which is called, ***The Four Noble Truth*** & *the* ***Noble Eightfold Path***.

The Four Noble Truths

1. There is Suffering. (*dukkha*).

2. Cause of Suffering. (*samudaya*).

3. End of Suffering Stop doing what causes suffering. (*nirodha*).

4. Path to end Suffering Everyone can be enlightened. (*marga*).

The Noble Eightfold Path

*1. **Right View**. The right way to think about life is to see the world through the eyes of the Buddha--with wisdom and compassion.*

*2. **Right Thinking**. We are what we think. Clear and kind thoughts build good, strong characters.*

*3. **Right Speech**. By speaking kind and helpful words, we are respected and trusted by everyone.*

*4. **Right Action**. No matter what we say, others know us from the way we behave. Before we criticize others, we should first see what we do ourselves.*

*5. **Right Livelihood**. This means choosing a job that does not hurt others. The Buddha said, "Do not earn your living by harming others. Do not seek happiness by making others unhappy."*

*6. **Right Effort**. A worthwhile life means doing our best at all times and having good will toward others. This also means not wasting effort on things that harm ourselves and others.*

*7. **Right Mindfulness**. This means being aware of our thoughts, words, and deeds.*

*8. **Right Concentration**. Focus on one thought or object at a time. By doing this, we can be quiet and attain true peace of mind.*

This is mathematics and regardless of orders one put forth the formulas, it simply adds to a mathematical scale from Knowledge to Born and Born back to the knowledge. Knowledge is "One" and Born is "Nine", and the foundation of this supreme order was done by Allah and his *Nine Borns*. He knew that the order of the numeral units were from 1 to 9, which was the month it took to be born into existence through the womb of the wisdom and that with the Arabic numeral cipher was the ending that knowledge came back to give the cipher value and made the knowledge infinite. When you place the knowledge before the cipher, you see the knowledge increase tenfold, and regardless to how many cipher the knowledge is before it gives value to the ciphers. And this is why the science of 19 is Savior in our Supreme Alphabets. So, Allah, Buddha, Moses, Christ and Muhammad were great elders who had different orders of their formulas, but each formula was a transformation of one's self. Otherwise, this is the school of God and the classroom of the Holy One; that which takes you into a higher enlightenment of self and the overpowering of the wisdom in the atmosphere. Whether Buddha or Allah, the teachings are similar and apparent to the consciousness of the wise. Allah truly is a man of divine understanding.

Who and what is the first "*Nine Borns*"? They were the first disciples of Allah in the person of Pudding. His first students were:

1. Kareem; 2. Black Messiah, 3. Nahim; a.k.a. Bismi Allah, 4. Uhuru, 5. Kihiem, 6. Al-Jabbar; a.k.a Prince Allah, 7. Al Jamel, Bilal Jihad and/or ABG 7; 8. Akbar 40 (Justice) and 9. Al Salaam.

Buddha also had five monks that he taught and Jesus had twelve disciples. And together they had 26 disciples which in the alphabet is the letter "Z", meaning <u>Zig Zag Zig</u>, meaning knowledge, wisdom and understanding. This is dealing with man, woman and children and that is who they had to go and teach these principles of life. After Buddha's enlightenment, he went to the Deer Park near the holy city of Benares and shared his new understanding with five monks. They understood immediately and became his disciples. This marked the beginning of his Buddhist community. However, he was not the first Buddha because there were scientist and wise men who predicted he would become a Buddha. This means they knew about Buddhism before Siddhartha Gautama knew the existence of Buddhism. W. D. Fard taught that Buddhism was 35,000 years old. 5020 - The first Buddha left the holy lands to teach Knowledge,

Wisdom, Understanding and the Culture, according to the 23rd Qur'an, within the Asiatic Calendar. So, Buddhism is really Islam and the principle of self-mastery. And you can see the similarity of the great and wise individuals whose persons Allah is present. Allah is the all eye seen, and is the product of pure intelligence. We do not see this as a mystery or a spook, but it is a living man. Man has the ability to become Allah or Buddha, through self-enlightenment. Even Gautama taught that he was not the first and would not be the last Buddha and that everyone has the capacity to become Buddha and so did Clarence 13 X—Allah. And this is how everything began with the 24 elders (Revelation 4:4).

Who are the twenty-four elders?

1. Jatu.
2. Zara.
3. Lukeman.
4. Wallah.
5. Mustafa.
6. Akill.
7. Mallah.
8. Salaam.
9. Jalah.
10. Ezeki-EL
11. Ahmed.
12. Talib.
13. Yacub
14. Akbar
15. Gabri-EL
16. Al Khalifa
17. Osmen Sharif
18. Rhmer
19. Sarmel
20. Rahman
21. Nabar
22. Jahear
23. Fard
24. Allah

Buddha also has other principles which are not mentioned in this chapter. But all the above is connected to the original man, who is the Kingdom of God, the maker, the owner, the cream of the planet earth and is actually God of the universe. If Allah is closest to you than your jugular veins, then this shows you that he starts with every original man. And this is why Buddha and Allah taught the mastery of self and the universe, regardless to what person or form he took or what body he came in. Allah is just man activated mentally and all ways possible in life, which means to overcome all situations in harmony in the universe, and this is the duty of all thinking individuals in the cipher to address the knowledge to a prescribe people to whom must be taught. In return he is the said person of that ability to teach all human families of the planet earth. Allah is always interested in the well-being of his people, and is the doctor of philosophy, meaning having power to heal the dumb, deaf and blind (Ph.D.). So when obtaining information you must be disciplined in applying to your everyday existence. Why should one get taught if he is not grateful or humble towards his teacher? So, each of you who are learnt, let your students be grateful and courteous to you or terminate his lessons or guidance. And this is the purpose Jesus predicted this verse, "**Give not that which is holy unto the dogs, neither cast ye your pearls before swine, lest they trample them under their feet, and turn again and rend you.**" (Matthew 7:6).

What is our duty to the Woman?

Just as any other, Justice is a scale of divine truth and power, so let us accumulate the knowledge of the cipher so that we can become the shapers of our own social equality. Thus, you have to clean a woman up to your perfection, so you can make her the Queen of your Kingdom, and to do this you must give her the knowledge of who and what is God. Once she is giving knowledge of your birth record and origin, she will be second in command in your universe, just as the universal flag of our nation, which consist of the sun, seven, moon and star. The flag is really your living social equality, because it represents reality, meaning man, woman and the child. A representation of aboriginal families, under the sun, moon and star; which is a completion of the universe. But after taking the woman to extensive studies of the black man, who is God, she has the power to help build a nation of righteousness, since she knowledge her man as God. Once this occurs she can be the Queen of God's Kingdom. After she is instructed with her understanding of the wisdom of God, she knows how to sew, cook, and in general how to act at home and abroad. And these are the training units that Allah (God) engages his woman to practice.

Ivan Van Sertima edited a book, Black Women in Antiquity, in which an article was written by Eloise McKinney-Johnson termed, "**Egypt's Isis: The Original Black Madonna**", pg. 64. She wrote:

"The great goddess Isis, 'The Lady of a Thousand Titles' is, like Cleopatra, her most illustrious devotee, a 'Great Enchantress' of infinite varieties. Some of her other titles are: 'Lady of

Heaven', 'Womanly Tenderness', 'Sisterly Love', Mistress of Magic', 'Lady of Light', 'Chamber-of-the-Birth-of-a-God' . . . "

Although, the Nation of God do not deal with the term Goddess, but if God is man and the opposite of God is devil, then she cannot be termed as a goddess, since she is in direct unity with her God. But just as long as we change the meaning of a goddess, which means a female Supreme Being and she and her God are supreme in the universe. How can you show me a being that is more supreme in intelligence than man and woman, male and female? So the term must be understood. Although, it was never taught or manifested in our teachings, but we can advance the meaning (Goddess) as being a co-instructor of the human family of the planet earth, and she is. We teach her how to act at home and abroad. But let us not get into fighting words over what it is, because you have the right to feel how you feel. It's your prerogative to see things as you see and not everyone will understand as such and have different rates of understanding. Otherwise, some are slower in mental capacity to others. Yet, to some you have not to explain, they readily understand on their own. Those are the ones that are at the mastery level. Let not the slow negative gases bring you down. Rather teach them at their level, meaning give them milk until you can give them meat. But the woman in our nation is known as the earth. We have the entire chapter in the Bible dedicated to the woman who knowledge God in the Proverbs. Let us place it.

Proverbs 31 (King James Version)

1 The words of king Lemuel, the prophecy that his mother taught him.

2 What, my son? And what, the son of my womb? And what, the son of my vows?

3 Give not thy strength unto women, nor thy ways to that which destroyeth kings.

4 It is not for kings, O Lemuel, it is not for kings to drink wine; nor for princes strong drink:

5 Lest they drink, and forget the law, and pervert the judgment of any of the afflicted.

6 Give strong drink unto him that is ready to perish, and wine unto those that be of heavy hearts.

7 Let him drink, and forget his poverty, and remember his misery no more.

8 Open thy mouth for the dumb in the cause of all such as are appointed to destruction.

9 Open thy mouth, judge righteously, and plead the cause of the poor and needy.

10 Who can find a virtuous woman? for her price is far above rubies.

11 The heart of her husband doth safely trust in her, so that he shall have no need of spoil.

12 She will do him good and not evil all the days of her life.

13 She seeketh wool, and flax, and worketh willingly with her hands.

14 She is like the merchants' ships; she bringeth her food from afar.

15 She riseth also while it is yet night, and giveth meat to her household, and a portion to her maidens.

16 She considereth a field, and buyeth it: with the fruit of her hands she planteth a vineyard.

17 She girdeth her loins with strength, and strengtheneth her arms.

18 She perceiveth that her merchandise is good: her candle goeth not out by night.

19 She layeth her hands to the spindle, and her hands hold the distaff.

20 She stretcheth out her hand to the poor; yea, she reacheth forth her hands to the needy.

21 She is not afraid of the snow for her household: for all her household are clothed with scarlet.

22 She maketh herself coverings of tapestry; her clothing is silk and purple.

23 Her husband is known in the gates, when he sitteth among the *elders* (24) of the land.

24 She maketh fine linen, and selleth it; and delivereth girdles unto the merchant.

25 Strength and honour are her clothing (3/4ths); and she shall rejoice in time to come.

26 She openeth her mouth with wisdom; and in her tongue is the law of kindness.

27 She looketh well to the ways of her household, and eateth not the bread of idleness.

28 Her children arise up, and call her blessed; her husband also, and he praiseth her.

29 Many daughters have done virtuously, but thou excellest them all.

30 Favour is deceitful, and beauty is vain: but a woman that feareth the Lord, she shall be praised.

31 Give her of the fruit of her hands; and let her own works praise her in the gates.

She knows that drinking will cause brothers to forget the laws of Islam and cause you to do other than righteousness and we're not speaking about mastering a thing like that. That is just an excuse to keep drinking that intoxicating drink. Real individual masters life, not drinking. You can tell when someone drinks, since he staggers through life and any one can take advantage of them. That's why the earth is the seed's first teacher. That is why you must teach her righteousness during her pregnancy. She gives birth do God, since she is the original Madonna. All the earths give birth to God. She was among the 5 women that kept the oil for the savior.

Matthew 25 (King James Version)

1Then shall the kingdom of heaven be likened unto ten virgins, which took their lamps, and went forth to meet the bridegroom.

2 And five of them were wise, and five were foolish.

3 They that were foolish took their lamps, and took no oil with them:

4 But the wise took oil in their vessels with their lamps.

5 While the bridegroom tarried, they all slumbered and slept.

6 And at midnight there was a cry made, Behold, the bridegroom cometh; go ye out to meet him.

7 Then all those virgins arose, and trimmed their lamps.

8 And the foolish said unto the wise, Give us of your oil; for our lamps are gone out.

9 But the wise answered, saying, Not so; lest there be not enough for us and you: but go ye rather to them that sell, and buy for yourselves.

10 And while they went to buy, the bridegroom came; and they that were ready went in with him to the marriage: and the door was shut.

11 Afterward came also the other virgins, saying, Lord, Lord, open to us.

12 But he answered and said, Verily I say unto you, I know you not.

13 Watch therefore, for ye know neither the day nor the hour wherein the Son of man cometh.

14 For the kingdom of heaven is as a man travelling into a far country, who called his own servants, and delivered unto them his goods (W.D. Fard). (Emphasis mines).

Thus the lessons says, "And no relief came until the Son of Man came to our aid, by the name of W.D. Fard", but this is who made us aware of the true and living God and our origin in this world. So, he taught Elijah Muhammad training units, which he called M.G.T. and G.C.C. Muslim Girl Training and General Civilization Classes are the training units, which consist of giving our black woman culture and awareness of knowledge, wisdom and understanding of a way of life:

- How to keep a home

- Sew
- Cook
- In general how to act at home and abroad.

W.D. Fard gave our Messenger these training regulations; to give our women culture and self-esteem; and bring forth beneficial result in their existence. This is how the woman acquires the ability to raise kings like Lemuel, through the wisdom of her God. King Lemuel was taught to attract a virtuous wife that is the embodiment of wisdom by his mother, such as Abigail, the bride of Nabal. *"Now the name of the man was Nabal; and the name of his wife Abigail: and she was a woman of good understanding, and of a beautiful countenance: but the man was churlish and evil in his doings; and he was of the house of Caleb."* (1 Samuel 25: 3). Jesus even speak well of these women who knowledge God, " "Verily I say unto you, Whosesoever this gospel shall be preached in the whole world, there shall also this, that this woman hath done, be told for a memorial of her." (Matthew 26:13). The earth massages her Savior, who is Allah, and makes him the King, whether he is her husband or her son. She is the Madonna. "Whoso findeth a wife findeth a good thing, and obtaineth favour of the Lord." (Proverbs 18:22). For the black woman is the natural bride of the black man, and is the only atmosphere where man can produce his nation in. "Therefore shall a man leave his father and his mother, and shall cleave unto his wife: and they shall be one flesh." (Gen. 2:24) Bi represents "two", and when you add a Cipher to the "Bi", it becomes Bio, which means "life", so they become one in life. Together, black man and woman: ". . . ye are a chosen generation, a royal priesthood, an holy nation, a peculiar people; that ye should shew forth the praises of him who hath called you out of darkness into his marvellous light." (1Petyer 2:9).

Together we are the life, which is the light and you must know the function of the earth within your cipher, which is a person, place or thing. Allah's teachings are present here to continue. A few years ago, you can hear the stupid remarks made by the 85%, who lacks self-knowledge, and now you see them giving their seeds righteous names, although they do not know what the meanings are; yet they are not selecting western names. Exactly what the Bible said about W.D. Fard.

Isaiah 65:15

And ye shall leave your name for a curse unto my chosen: for the Lord God shall slay thee, and call his servants by another name.

Thus, while building God, you are destroying devil, because once God is birthed you are destroying devil since he has no power over the righteous or God. Just as the Qur'an is taught, "And He it is Who created the heavens and the earth in accordance with the requirements of wisdom; and the day He says, 'Be!' it will be. His word is the truth, and His will be the kingdom on the day when the trumpet will be blown. He is the Knower of the unseen and the seen. And He is the Wise, the All-Aware." (Al-An`am Chapter 6: Verse 74). The Qur'an also states that in the presence of the truth, falsehood would vanish and the Nation of Gods and earths calls this ***Build or Destroy***. Build is to add on and destroy is to take away. The father is one (knowledge) who "Fat"-"her" (wisdom) and bring forth the child or seed into being (understanding), which is known as Zig Zag Zig. Therefore his blueprint is for his wisdom (woman) to reflect his light and shine the light back to the children in their cipher like our universal flag, which is in front of all my books. Thus, the queen may bring forth the God from her womb, mentally as well as physically. A cycle of righteousness is our functions, and you can bear witness to the truth and it can be presented in all the scriptures that we are the said people of that ability, who are held responsible for teaching the truth. We are going to the truth in the Holy Qur'an and the Bible and see what it means for us as a nation.

Some of you claim that you do not deal with religion, but let us go into that. How are you going to claim this when we are to teach civilization to others and those are the people that we have to teach--the seeds of Abraham? Jews, Christians and Muslims are to be saved and brought together for one common cause; to make a nation of Gods and earths, under the banner of freedom, justice and equality (Islam). Remember the promise made to Abraham by Allah about the city (Mecca), and he would have his seeds become Imams. An imam means a righteous teacher. And we are the examples of that teacher, shaped by the Messenger Elijah Muhammad, in the person of Allah by Clarence Smith 13X, known as ***Pudding.*** Knowing and understanding 120 lessons of life and showing our leadership for all the nations, Jew-Arab and all the people of Abraham. For, black man, is the father of all human beings on the planet. Just by understanding the DNA of the black man, you know that he is the ***One Blood*** in the Bible that is the prototype to shape after himself, ". . . **all nations of men for to dwell on all the face of the earth, and hath determined the times before appointed, and the bounds of their habitation;**" (Acts 17:26). We decided that it would take six hundred years to make him, and ran him over the Hot Arabian Desert, into the caves of West Asia, as they now call it "Europe". According to Elijah "Eu" means "Hillside" and "Rope" means the "Rope" to bind in, as taught to him by Allah in the person of W.D. Fard. Thus, we knew the "bounds of their habitation", and he stayed there and lived like a savage for two thousand years. They (devil) were not making history for themselves until Musa came to civilize them and remind them of their duty to their Lord (Yacub or Musa). So, the earth belongs to the original man, so we must claim back our woman and clean her up of the filth that white man has corrupted her with. Habakkuk 2:14 says, "**For the earth shall be filled with the knowledge of the glory of the Lord, as the waters cover the sea.**"

I have fought the good fight, I have finished the race, I have kept the faith. Finally, there is laid up for me the crown of righteousness, which the Lord, the righteous Judge, will give to me on that Day, and not to me only but also to all who have loved ***His appearing***. --2 Timothy 4:7-8

He did appear if you think he is a mystery. If he did not have a body how could he have made an appearance? He is quite a man. One having 360° of knowledge, Alpha and Omega. I am proving right now that I am Allah, One who has given the world civilization, righteousness and the knowledge of themselves, love, peace and happiness. For I am, "***Father of civilization and God of the universe***." This is what our father taught us. When it comes to being God, no one stress this more than the NGE, Nation of Gods and earths.

Truth within the Scriptures

Holy Quran: The City

90:1

I do call to witness this City;-

90:2

And thou art a freeman of this City;-

90:3

And (the mystic ties of) parent and child;-

90:4

Verily We have created man into toil and struggle.

90:5

Thinketh he, that none hath power over him?

90:6

He may say (boastfully); Wealth have I squandered in abundance!

90:7

Thinketh he that none beholdeth him?

90:8

Have We not made for him a pair of eyes?-

90:9

And a tongue, and a pair of lips?-

90:10

And shown him the two highways?

90:11

But he hath made no haste on the path that is steep.

90:12

And what will explain to thee the path that is steep?-

90:13

(It is:) freeing the bondman;

90:14

Or the giving of food in a day of privation

90:15

To the orphan with claims of relationship,

90:16

Or to the indigent (down) in the dust.

90:17

Then will he be of those who believe, and enjoin patience, (constancy, and self-restraint), and enjoin deeds of kindness and compassion.

90:18

Such are the Companions of the Right Hand.

90:19

But those who reject Our Signs, they are the (unhappy) Companions of the Left Hand.

90:20

On them will be Fire vaulted over (all round).

The city spoken about here is the Holy city of Mecca, which is where the knowledge and wisdom of the original man first started when the planet was first founded. It is known in the scriptures as Mt. Paran. "***God came from Teman, and the Holy One from mount Paran. Selah. His glory covered the heavens, and the earth was full of his praise.***" (Habakkuk 3:3)

2 Peter 3:10 (King James Version)

But the day of the Lord will come as a thief in the night*; in the which the heavens shall pass away with a great noise, and the elements shall melt with fervent heat, the earth also and the works that are therein shall be burned up.*

However, God came from the east to the West, then, **HQ. 90:1** is relating to a city or cities in the west as well. Fard made Elijah a free man from ignorance and mental death. "And the mystic ties of parent and child" is the duty of Elijah turning the hearts of the children to the father and the father to the children, and it states clearly in the Bible, **Malachi 4:6**: "**And he shall turn the heart of the fathers to the children, and the heart of the children to their fathers, lest I come and smite the earth with a curse**." You see the storms that we are getting when the Son of man made his appearance, taught his messenger; and we who are scholars, scientist and knowers of the teachings of Elijah recognize the changes taken place in the general atmosphere (earth), and we are the cause of this. All above is caused by the Son of man. If you do not agree, why did Jesus said,

Luke 17:6

And the Lord said, If ye had faith as a grain of mustard seed, ye might say unto this sycamine tree, Be thou plucked up by the root, and be thou planted in the sea; and it should obey you.

Thus, he is telling you that the kingdom of God is right within you and you can say "Be" and it "become" whatever you ordered it to become. He explained it to his disciples and said it in different details that he is the original man, and "God of the universe." But like the Qur'an says, we made him toil, hasty and with the will to master the original people, so it is hard to get Caucasians to submit to the black man's rules and regulations, or the law of righteousness. His ways and actions are like those of a snake. All the prophets who came tried to reform him (devil) and were unable to. So we have decided that it cannot be done and he cannot go back in the womb of his mother, so he cannot be grafted back in any amount of time or years, months and days. The only way would be to take him off the planet. But he would take his own self off the planet. He is a dare devil and will kill himself quickly instead of facing justice. This is why the Bible calls him a serpent, because he has no back bone. Not to omit, a fugitive and a vagabond. He has committed so many crimes against nature that he is afraid, when we learn about him; we will run him from among us. This is a fact, and it is well documented in the history of the earth's civilization, especially by the maker and owner of the universe.

We have given those (85%) knowledge and the eyes to see, yet they reject knowledge and boast about how much money they have. Your wealth will not save you from your wicked ways in the hereafter. If you come up with something other than the truth, it won't be accepted. Even Jesus said to be accepted you have to have the righteousness of the Jew. The Jew does not eat pork, he follows the laws of righteousness and do not bear false witness. The path that is steep is freeing the dumb, by educating him, making him see, hear and speak the words of God; who is Allah. There are those who are in the right hand and those on the left hand. This is referring with the two people who represent each other, who the prophet Moses will be compared with, who will be one like him and he will teach a people who are similar with the ones in Egypt. So the one who represent this will separate the two people and one on the right hand would be the sheep and the one in the left would be the goat, which represents the two characteristics of the two people. But the sheep are, "Such are the Companions of the Right Hand." (HQ. 90:18).

Yet, those who reject our signs are the goat, which shows the characteristics the Caucasian man, first and last. The proto-type; and the carbon copy, the last stage in the book of genetic (Revelation). And this is his destruction when you get to Revelation. He is the same serpent in the beginning of Genesis and the ending in Revelation.

Holy Qur'an 90:19

But those who reject Our Signs, they are the (unhappy) Companions of the Left Hand.

However, just like we are living like in the days of Noah, it is no different when he saw the coming of destruction and this is a warning to all people or human beings on the earth, respect the chosen people of God and his nation of Gods and earths.

Matthew 24:37-38 (NASV)

"But as the days of Noah were, so shall also the coming of the Son of man be . . . For as in the days that were before the flood they were eating and drinking, marrying and giving in marriage, until the day that Noah entered into the ark."

Conclusion

The Judgment

But when the Son of Man comes in His glory, and all the angels with Him, then He will sit on His glorious throne . . .All the nations will be gathered before Him; and He will separate them from one another, as the shepherd separates the sheep from the goats. . .and He will put the sheep on His right, and the goats on the left. . .Then the King will say to those on His right, Come, you who are blessed of My Father, inherit the kingdom prepared for you from the foundation of the world. . .For I was hungry, and you gave Me something to eat; I was thirsty, and you gave Me something to drink; I was a stranger, and you invited Me in . . . naked, and you clothed Me; I was sick, and you visited Me; I was in prison, and you came to Me . .

.Then the righteous will answer Him, Lord, when did we see You hungry, and feed You, or thirsty, and give You something to drink . . . And when did we see You a stranger, and invite You in, or naked, and clothe You. . . When did we see You sick, or in prison, and come to You . . . The King will answer and say to them, Truly I say to you, to the extent that you did it to one of these brothers of Mine, even the least of them, you did it to Me. . . Then He will also say to those on His left, Depart from Me, accursed ones, into the eternal fire which has been prepared for the devil and his angels. . . for I was hungry, and you gave Me nothing to eat; I was thirsty, and you gave Me nothing to drink. . . I was a stranger, and you did not invite Me in; naked, and you did not clothe Me; sick, and in prison, and you did not visit Me . . . then they themselves also will answer, Lord, when did we see You hungry, or thirsty, or a stranger, or naked, or sick, or in prison, and did not take care of You. . .Then He will answer them, Truly I say to you, to the extent that you did not do it to one of the least of these, you did not do it to Me. . .These will go away into eternal punishment, but the righteous into eternal life. (Matthew 25-31-46).

Fard taught Elijah, "He likes the devil because the devil gives him nothing", but only gifts that blinds the eyes, causing our people to be unaware of the Messiah or one who represents Allah. So, Allah represents those who needs bread and are needy. So, we won't be lied to, after knowledge of ourselves, or be fooled when understanding mathematics. We'll never believe in those who teaches us that God is mysterious; who are from *that nation* which God shall judge. Also we are beaten and killed by the same ones who advocate this type of God, and they knowing themselves that there are no God other than man. He keeps us blind so that he can master us. He desires to make slaves (mentally) out of all he can so he can rob us and live in a luxury.

Always know that Allah is God, always has been and always will be. Holy Qur'an 23:78-79: *"It is He Who has created for you (the faculties of) hearing, sight, feeling and understanding: little thanks it is ye give . . . And He has multiplied you."*

Some of the brothers who are Jews, Christians and Muslims ask us if we are God, how did we create the earth, but how can they ask that if we say in the Qur'an "Be" and it is? Recently the CBS announced, "Physicists in Italy said

Wednesday (3/12/2013) they are achingly close to concluding that what they found last year was the Higgs boson, the elusive 'God particle.' They need to eliminate one last remote possibility that it's something else."

Elijah said that the black man is self-created and here is scientist coming closer to what the Elijah Muhammad taught. European Center for Nuclear Research is just finding out today what Elijah taught in the 1930's. Scientists are closer to being certain they found what they call the crucial "Higgs boson", which they co-termed "God particle". This they claim to be the key to the universe. This is showing you today that white man (Caucasians) is on his job showing you that he can prove the existence of Elijah's teachings. He does not deny Elijah, but just try to write him out of his existence, since he never wanted a black Messiah to open the eyes of the people, under the King Alfred plan and the Willie Lynch mentality; as well as the mentality of Arnold Toynbee. However, Peter Higgs paid close attention to the teachings of Elijah Muhammad, who said we were self-created as the original man on the planet, and that we are the atom, Allah the original man, which gave the sparks of burning gases which was the helium and the hydrogen. Elijah did not have a college degree, just a third grade education, but confounded the scientists of the world. You witness this in Elijah himself, his ministers, students and disciples. Malcolm, Farrakhan, and Clarence 13X, The NOI, NGE and many scholars from our biological roots. This "God particle" was also predicted in 1964, the same year Allah born his nation, and this is indeed a sign for those who understand. There are many signs to show the Son of man coming from the heavens with great science and glory, meaning that he is coming from above just as Jesus, and not beneath. Meaning we are not of this world of Adam, but the father of Adamites and all other human beings. The entire world is after our existence.

However, Leon Lederman is the one who named it The "God Particle", but Allah wouldn't allow the forces of nature to let him name his book (The God Particle) by his first idea for the name of the said book, which he wanted to name "The Goddam Particle". Allah forced his publisher to change the name. So, this is the footprint of God in the universe. Thus, this was the teachings of God. The devils put the truth in hidden forms and if ignorant of the truth; in which he has no will to put among black people, and this is why Fard gave Elijah an Arabic Qur'an and told Elijah to read it and Elijah said he couldn't read it, and Fard told him when he learn the Arabic, he would give Elijah the English one. Why is it so important to have the Arabic Qur'an written or translated into English? Because the people of God had to be reached in order to lift them up. Fard did not go to the rich people of the land, but deep down in the Ghettos (Ghettoes) of Detroit. We did not speak our own language anymore, but only spoke the languages of our Western slave makers. This is why **Isaiah 29:11-12**, says:

11 **And the vision of all is become unto you as the words of a book that is sealed, which men deliver to one that is learned, saying, Read this, I pray thee: and he saith, I cannot; for it is sealed**:

12 **And the book is delivered to him that is not learned, saying, Read this, I pray thee: and he saith, I am not learned**.

And the Holy Qur'an bears witness that Muhammad Ibn Abdullah was a sign ending prophecy of the east and for one who will be beginning of the west, Alpha and Omega, to show and prove that Allah is the black man, always has been and always will be. That one will restore all things and bring back God to the cipher. He will not recognize same sex marriages, the eating of swine's flesh and will not be guided or be fooled by the devil's psychology and trick-knowledge. Just as Jesus told the devil about his evil affairs on the planet and showed and proved taught he was of his' father the "devil". There was no physical book for Muhammad to read, so how can he read it, especially if he died not knowing how to read it. The Honorable Elijah Muhammad (THEM) knew how to read English, but not Arabic, although he only had a third grade education. But W.D. Fard gave him the Arabic Qur'an that Fard wrote himself. But Elijah could not read that and the Qur'an says:

Surah 96. The Clot, Read!

1. Proclaim! (Or read!) In the name of thy Lord and Cherisher, Who created-

2. Created man, out of a (mere) clot of congealed blood:

3. Proclaim! And thy Lord is Most Bountiful,-

4. He Who taught (the use of) the pen,-

5. Taught man that which he knew not.

6. Nay, but man doth transgress all bounds,

7. In that he looketh upon himself as self-sufficient.

8. Verily, to thy Lord is the return (of all).

9. Seest thou one who forbids-

10. A votary when he (turns) to pray?

11. Seest thou if he is on (the road of) Guidance?-

12. Or enjoins Righteousness?

13. Seest thou if he denies (Truth) and turns away?

14. Knoweth he not that Allah doth see?

15. Let him beware! If he desist not, We will drag him by the forelock,-

16. A lying, sinful forelock!

17. Then, let him call (for help) to his council (of comrades):

18. We will call on the angels of punishment (to deal with him)!

19. Nay, heed him not: But bow down in adoration, and bring thyself closer (to Allah.)!

So, this was the vision that Muhammad had in the caves, when the Angel Gabriel told him to read, he ran home to his wife, petrified, which was a vision for Elijah to snatch the book from the one on the throne, who is Allah. Although Muhammad was inspired to memorize this miracle, he could not write it or read it. So, let us go into the Qur'an and prove this greatness that only Allah could show and prove and I am He. This was done in the 27th of the month of Ramadan, before the Qur'an was in written form. He was in the cave known as Mount Hira, in the year 610. Mount Hira is known as *The Mountain of Light,* which is located in the Hejaz region of present day Saudi Arabia in Mekkah (Mecca); when he heard words in the vision saying "Iqra", meaning "Read" and "Recite". And if you claim that it was an angel called Gabriel, thus; he was a man since Gabriel appeared to Marie as a well-made man to represent the spirit of Allah in the 19th Chapter of Qur'an. Yet, there are 19 verses in this Surah known as the Clot of Congealed Blood. Do you see the relationship? However, Surah 19 has 98 ayat (verses), and the last two tells us,

97. "**So have We made the (Qur'an) easy in thine own tongue**, that with it thou mayest give Glad Tidings to the righteous, and warnings to people given to contention.

98. But how many (countless) generations before them have We destroyed? Canst thou find a single one of them (now) or hear (so much as) a whisper of them?"

You subtract two from 98 and you are left with 96, and this is the solution to the mathematical equation. (96 and 96)*, which is the first Chapter of the Qur'an that we gave to Muhammad ibn Abdullah. And then Allah wrote it to address all the seeds of Abraham and the lost-found in the wilderness of North America. Even in the Isra and Mi'raj, According to report of Malik ibn Sa'sa'ah, "Moses said: 'I weep because of a young man sent after me, whose *Ummah* will enter Paradise in greater numbers than mine." This vision of Muhammad is telling you of Elijah, since Elijah taught more years than Muhammad ibn Abdullah. T.H.E.M lasted and lived longer than Muhammad of 1400 years ago and the latter was a sign for Elijah, who promised that his culture would supersede all others. Let us go into the next chapter and prove this. We made the Qur'an easy in his own tongue (Arabic), but it belongs to us, it's a confirmation of earlier scriptures, so Prophet Muhammad had limited light of the Qur'an or could not tell you all the science of it until one who was taught by *one mighty in power* would come. So let us chase this on the next chapter called "Check Mate to all Falsehood and Denials." * 96X2= 192-1877= 1865, which deals with A. Lincoln.

Check mate to all Falsehood and Denials

Remember in my first book <u>*Revelation of the God from the Ghettoes of Hell* in the Body of the 5%</u>? I wrote, "Master Fard made his appearance in and out of America in the 1920s. When he first made his appearance among black people was in July 4th, 1930. At least 154 years after the Independence of the USA. *154* represent significant things in Islam. He came within 154 years after America got independence from Britain. When you subtract 10 from 154 you are left with 144, since he came with the Student Enrollment and he do represent the 10, one before the cipher. Cipher is a person, place or thing. He is the one who has come before the world, so you subtract the 10 from the 154 and you get 144. Why 144? He is sent to his chosen ones—144,000 man, woman and children. "And I heard the number of them which were sealed: and there were sealed an hundred and forty and four thousands of all the tribes of the children of Israel." (Rev. 7:4).

The Revelation says, ". . . He measured the wall thereof, an hundred and forty and four cubits, according to the measure of ***a man***, that is, of the angel. [This is the measure of Master Fard]. Emphasis mines.

Did not Muhammad say he was approached by an angel Gabriel? What is the meaning of Gabriel? Gabriel means *man of God.* The Pictorial Bible Dictionary says, "**He is mentioned *Four* times in Scripture, each time bearing a momentous message. He interpreted to Daniel the vision of the ram and the he-goat (Dan 8:16f). In Daniel 9:21f he explained the vision of the 70 Weeks. Gabriel announced to Zacharias the birth of John, forerunner of the Messiah (Luke 1:11-20), and he was sent to Mary with the unique message of Jesus' birth (Luke 1:26-38). His preparation is the ideal for every messenger of God: 'I am Gabriel, that stand in the presence of God; and am sent to speak unto thee' (Luke 1:19). The Bible does not define his angel-status, but he appears in the Book of Enoch (chs. 9, 20, 40) as an archangel.**"

Now let us go to the Book of Enoch and see what these mentioned chapters above are saying. For it was originally written in the Afro-asiatic language of

Ethiopic and translated into English. Let us understand what is said in all scriptures.

Chapter 9:

1 And then Michael, Uriel, Raphael, and Gabriel looked down from heaven and saw much blood being

2 shed upon the earth, and all lawlessness being wrought upon the earth. And they said one to another: 'The earth made without inhabitant cries the voice of their cryingst up to the gates of heaven.

3 And now to you, the holy ones of heaven, the souls of men make their suit, saying, "Bring our cause

4 before the Most High."' And they said to the Lord of the ages: 'Lord of lords, God of gods, King of kings, and God of the ages, the throne of Thy glory (standeth) unto all the generations of the

5 ages, and Thy name holy and glorious and blessed unto all the ages! Thou hast made all things, and power over all things hast Thou: and all things are naked and open in Thy sight, and Thou seest all

6 things, and nothing can hide itself from Thee. Thou seest what Azazel hath done, who hath taught all unrighteousness on earth and revealed the eternal secrets which were (preserved) in heaven, which

7 men were striving to learn: And Semjaza, to whom Thou hast given authority to bear rule over his associates.

8. And they have gone to the daughters of men upon the earth, and have slept with the women, and have defiled themselves, and revealed to them all kinds of sins.

9. And the women have borne giants, and the whole earth has thereby been filled with blood and unrighteousness.

For man is God; and tittles are given to characters, prophets and are but manifestation of man and woman—male and female. This is not saying if you are defined by these tittles that you are not God. Man is God, since he was made to be the ruler on the earth and he is made to execute the commandment of the Almighty true and living God. Thus, man holds a high position on the earth, and this is not to practice chauvinisms, but to apply Godly principles on the earth. That is to apply judgment of God on the ungodly upon the earth. Thus, if this is the Days of Allah, the judgment Day or the Days of Resurrections, then you must apply the judgment of God to all situations and this is with righteousness and not with a corrupt heart or contaminated intelligence. You must deal with the Omnipotent and re-collective mind. A man must keep his Sabbath sacred, meaning keep his Days of Divinity from being mixed up, diluted and tampered within any form. This is what makes one original, meaning having knowledge, wisdom, understanding, culture, refinement and is not a savage in the pursuit of happiness. He has no twofold of double in any form. Then will you behold righteousness reign on the planet, which the Holy Qur'an acknowledge by saying that this way of life will supersede all other religion, but yet this is not a religion.

For one's way of living to supersede all others is the position only Allah holds. Why? Allah is Most High with knowledge, wisdom and understanding. If his way did not overcome he would not be Allah. But do not think Allah is a special name that no one can attain. Allah is but a Semitic name for the Supreme Being. So, it holds no special powers different of God or the all in all. He is not unseen; he is seen and heard everywhere, for he is the all-eye-seeing. Otherwise, he is a substance of pure intelligence. But at certain times in the universe he appears as a person who brings forth changes for the next 25,000 years. He is known as a builder, supreme architect and the one to whom all praises is due. He is independent of the world that exists 20 miles outside his righteousness. He is the executer of divine culture and represents the sun of righteousness. His knowledge represents 360° of numeral units, known as the science of everything in life, and Supreme Mathematics; love, peace and happiness. And this is the blueprint of God. After this world of 6,000 years, is the bringing forth of the Sabbath Day, the Days of Allah, the Ressurection Day and the beginning of a new cycle. That cycle is the destruction of the devil's civilization. So, one day is like 1,000 years to the Lord. After the 6 day, when Jesus' showed the transfiguration of the three speaking, as I put on page 14. It represented the 6,000 years.

You have witness president Obama say that Trayvon Martin could have been his son. He was shot by Zimmerman who was following the young God. The young God had to defend himself and he only had a bag of Skittles and an ice tea. He shot the young God point blank, and they say he was not guilty of murder. Right there they are showing that they do not care about our president and showing disrespect toward the black community. But this is a continuous stage in the black man's history in North America. Could this be a sign from the forces of nature that it is enforcing the law of separation from the enemies of God? They do not love God or his righteousness, and will not keep and obey the laws of Islam or the commandments of God. Many black people have claimed self-defense in cases that they did harm to people and were convicted. Here Zimmerman claims that (self-defense) and he went looking for trouble, following the young God and murdered the young God and got acquitted and they gave him back his gun. Meaning that it is all right to kill black men, and you will not get arrested. So, we have to pay close attention to that. But let us go back to W.D. Fard now.

Now the Bible said he would come as a thief in the night, in 2 Peter 3:10. Also said it would be "Fervent heat" on that day. Let us put the verse so we can identify what it says, just like on page 78.

But the day of the Lord will come as a thief in the night; in the which the heavens shall pass away with a great noise, and the elements shall melt with *fervent heat*, the earth also and the works that are therein *shall be burned up*.

This is stating that the temperature will be hot on his arrival, so let us see what the temperature was at that time. He came in 1930, and his coming was in Detroit. So, let us go see if it was hot and burning in that year.

The Heat is On: A look at 100F+ temps & heat waves in Detroit, MI

Started By Michsnowfreak: 26 Jun 2012 11:51 AM.

First here's a decadal breakdown. The 1930s-50s stick out like a sore thumb, and the heat of that 30-year period is probably even more impressive than the lack of snow which occurred in that same timeframe (ohhh what a field day warmingistas would have if such conditions occurred now ;))

Detroit has hit 100F+ just 37 times since records began in 1871. Yes, they have hit 99F numerous additional times as well, but officially, that is no more a 100F reading than a 5.9" snowfall is a 6"+ storm.

...............90F+........100F+

1900s ----- 56 times --- 0 times

1910s --- 107 times --- 3 times

1920s --- 100 times --- 0 times *est due to M 1923 data

1930s --- 172 times --- 14 times

1940s --- 160 times --- 2 times

1950s --- 154 times --- 5 times

1960s --- 111 times --- 0 times

1970s --- 119 times --- 2 times

1980s --- 127 times --- 5 times

1990s --- 123 times --- 1 time

2000s --- 102 times --- 0 times

2010s ----- 64 times --- 4 times *thru 7/2012

As you see that 1930 had the hottest days than all the other years. Why? It was the coming of the Lord. In 1930 the temperature of 90F+ was recorded 172 times and 100+ 14 times. More than any other year and this is about the time of the great depression. So, he tells you records begin before the birth of Master Fard, which was in 1877, and this was 6 years before his birth (1871). It was manifested by nature, to begin recording the forecast for this day, to show and prove his existence as the Son of man. Thus, since he taught all of us to be Allah, then he gets the credit, since he was the one they spoke in the Bible who would come. No one can take this from him. It is proven in all types of ways, from the forecast to his presence in the wilderness of North America. And again, you have the number six (6) come up. Six days before he was born, which was to also begin recording the forecast for the preparation of the Son of man to mark the six thousand years of the devil being birthed on the planet. He is the truth and our foundation is from him. He came in the form so that he can go by both people and give this knowledge to Elijah, so Elijah can give it to us and he would come again on his 87th birthday as Put, aka Pudding, known as Father Allah. So, six days later Jesus show his disciple the vision of Elijah, then 6 years before Fard's birth was the recording of the forecast. In this is understanding for the wise and guidance for the righteous. It is proven every which way that the Master Fard's teaching is right and exact as taught by Allah in person, and we are Allah. We are one in the body of the 5%. That ***One Blood*** in the Bible is us. We say "Let Us make man".

So, we have to make man in our likeness and make the circumference of our children's education equal to ours, just like Elijah was to turn the hearts of the children to their father and the father's to the children. We have to continue the teachings and build with every available factor within our reach and within our environments. The lessons are a blessing to keep us from guessing. We do not guess at a thing. We deal with actual and natural facts and we have a blueprint right within our DNA. We must deal with the Evolution of the original man. He must be greater than he has been in the past centuries. So, we must approach this century with the will of Allah, masterful and with vigilance and protection of our biological roots. Black man is God, always has been and always will be. We must approach everything as a master. For it is our time to make a stand. Like Yacub gave his orders to the colored man, "Be fruitful, and multiply, and replenish the earth, and subdue it: and have dominion over the fish of the sea, and over the fowl of the air, and over every living thing that moveth upon the earth." (Gen. 1:28).

Now that we know the blueprint of God, then perform responsibly your interest for the mastery of self and the universe and claim your divinity as the maker and owner, the cream of the planet earth and God of the universe. This is the Days of the Asiatic black man, so whether black, brown and yellow you must unite and make a stand. Even Caucasians who respect righteousness we have nothing against you, just teach truth to your people and make them respect their fathers and mothers, Gods and earths. We respect all the human families of the planet earth, but we record the history of people's behavior on the earth and we know your history, so there is no need to cover up your history because we made you and know about your filthy affairs on the planet. We know about your desire with the same sex lust and so-called marriage, which is an abomination unto God. The Qur'an says, "Allah's commandment will come to pass, so seek not to hasten it. Glory be to him, and highly exalted be he above what they associate (with him)!" (HQ. 15:1). Look at what George G.M. James had to say about us, the Gods.

"The Gods of Order and arrangement in the cosmos are represented by nine gods, in one God-head, called the Ennead. Here Atum (Atom), the source of the Ogload, is also retained as the source of the Gods of Order and arrangement.

Atum (Atom) names four pairs of parts of his own body, and thus creates eight Gods, who together with himself become nine. These Eight Gods are created Gods, the first creatures of this world; and Atum (Atom), the Creator God, the Demiurge, of who Plato spoke. The Gods whom Atum (Atom) projected from his body were

(i) Shu (Air)
(ii) Tefnut (Moisture)
(iii) Geb (Earth)
(iv) Nut (Sky);

Who are said to have given birth to four other Gods:

(v) Osiris (the God of omnipotence and omniscience)
(vi) Isis (wife of Osiris, Female Principle)
(vii) Seth (the opposite of good)
(viii) Nephthys (Female Principle in the Unseen World).

(Plutarch: Isis et Osiris, 355 A; 364 C; 371B; Frankfurt; Intellectual Adventure of Ancient Man, p. 66-67)." –Stolen Legacy, pp. 142-143, by George G.M. James. So, you can see why that the messenger spoke about us being self-created when speaking upon the black man. He said we were from the Asiatic Tribe of Shabbazz. So, we have to come together and get our children prepared so we can execute this blueprint as the Gods of the universe. Allah says in the Bible, "Behold, I make all things new", so we have to renew history and make everything bow down to the truth by teaching and reciting our history or Qur'an. And you conscious black man whose mind function at the speed of light (186,000 miles per seconds) can already see this and understand the revelation.

Nowadays, the devil is still performing unrighteous functions and are still scattered on various poor parts of the planet earth and are continuing to deal with different levels of grafted mentality on the earth; and thus trying to impose their wickedness on those he has planted fear within. The result is separation from the wise from the dumb. The devil causes a division among the original people, through names and labels. And you are all going for it. Is he planting fear in you now that you are a grown man? Can a devil fool a righteous man? Can a devil fool God? He cannot fool the Elijah Muhammad's Nation of Islam, but I think he can fool the Arab Muslims. Why? The devil is using the same principles he used to break up the rise of the black people in the wilderness of North America in the east, where the original man's knowledge first was founded. He must be check mated and wherever he is at challenge him and his government. Challenge everything the devil throw at you and you will see that when he cannot handle you he will shout his mouth and will back away. By nature he looks for the Messiah in the black man, just as they did in the days of Moses and Jesus that they wanted to kill all the sons. Well, Trayvon Martin case is telling you that you can kill black sons of man and there will be no justice. Thus, we have to get our own justice. Be bold and be not afraid to give your life. Ali lost all he had to stand up for his right, and made a good sacrifice in which he won and gain national recognition for his greatness. He stood against the government and won. How many of you have that courage? Just rise up Son of man. They know the power is within you so they are hateful towards you and we are their parents. We really are not worried about them because we can take power from them anytime we get ready to, regardless of how much military powers he may claim to have. All this is meaningless to God.

You are not giving W.D. Fard proper respect because you take his presence lightly. He is a scientist, God that was self-taught, independent, meaning came by himself. He did not care about the oppressor and came solely for the black man. Well, we have this knowledge and we have not been taught that by the orthodox Muslims, nor did the Caucasian man give us that education. We received these lessons from W.D. Fard. These training units were given to us by W.D. Fard. And no relief came to us until the Son of man came to our aid by the name of W.D, Fard. So, if the father did not agree to that he would have changed that and would not have given us 120 lessons. So, many of you who are speaking about Fard is half original man, you shout your mouths because you justify that you are not pro-black nor anti-white, so why are you throwing the devil's argument about Fard BEING a white man? You don't know history and are poorly educated. All in the Qur'an and Bible is the science you can see the existence of the Son of man. That is a tittle exclusive to W.D. Fard. He was on time and his Messenger as well. You disagree with one you disagree with the other. And he did not teach Elijah to get the money and here's my address. He told Elijah I must now leave you. So the bible fills you with the teachings of who the son of man is. He is Allah in person just like everyone of us. Every description fits him and proves him. He came quietly and the world knew him not. Only his student-Messenger knew him. I know him and I study him and I study myself. Therefore, we must study and really find evidence of the teachings, so we can checkmate all evil of the world. The game of chess is like a sword fight. You must first think before you move. And it's a battle between good and bad. It's a jihad in the mental. A jihad is right within you, just as the kingdom of God, which is a Sabbath, the Day of God, and this is the Blueprint of God. So, bear witness to the truth and turn not from it and like Jesus said worship in spirit and in truth. For only the truth shall set you free. Abraham Lincoln won't set you free, the Supreme Court won't set you free, and it's only the truth that will set you free. And this is the truth that the Son of Man brought to us as a whole. All praises due to Allah, Lord of all the worlds. There is no God but Allah and Elijah Muhammad is the last and final messenger.

But if you examine the teachings of W.D. Fard once again you will see that he is God, especially with the Problem Book, since he gets into the science of how many cubic of air that you breathe your entire life. He can tell you how much water is in the ocean and how many pounds of water are there. By the population of a town he can explain to you how much pound the people weigh along with town's area square mileage. He was able to tell you how, what, when, where, which and all things through a mathematical precision, which you can see through his problem book, and by observing such he wanted for us to be the absolute rulers of the earth and ourselves. I do not know the reason that the father Allah did not give us the problem book, but I think it is necessary for the true and living to know that science, so that our brain power would be at its fullest. All minds are necessitated to remain sharp and that is a proper and beneficial practice of the mind. For the mind is a terrible thing to waste. But most of the students of the father were seeds, so it could be that he thought the Problem book where to high of a science for them, so he kept that out until he can give it to them at a later date. By knowing the problem book, you are completely in control of self and in self-mastery. For example, the fourth (4th) lesson in the Problem Book says: "One one-hundredth of a cubic inch contains two hundred million Atoms. How many will fifty square miles contain?" So, one have to calculate what the answer is through knowledge of what kind of measurement and calculation to apply. Just as the fifth (5th) lesson says or asks:

"The uncle of Mr. W.D. Fard lives in the wilderness of North America and he is living other than himself, therefore, he weighs more than his height and his blood pressure registers more than thirty-two. This killed him at the age of forty-four years. The average person breathes three cubic feet of air per hour, but the uncle of Mr. W.D. Fard breathes three and seven-tenths of a cubic foot per hour. How many cubic feet of air did Mr. W.D. Fard's uncle breathe in forty-four years? How many Atoms does he breathe in all of his forty-four years when one one-hundredth of a cubic inch contains two hundred million Atoms?"

This shows you that Allah is God, because a lot of you wouldn't even think so deeply and wouldn't even know this was possible for you to know, so always respect the author of the lessons that we call 120° of life, also known as what the NOI calls Supreme Wisdom. So, this knowledge is not a joke and is very realistic and one have to continue daily to keep studying and teach what has come to him from the result of experimenting with the high science. Thus, we deal with the high intellectual frequencies to the utmost precision. In 1991, Muammar Al Quaddafi wrote The Green Book, and this is also a book to contribute to our growth and development. He gives his views on Solution of the democracy, economic problems and social basis of the Third Universal Theory. This is what the publisher had to say about his book:

"The thinker Muammar Al QUADDAFI does not present his thought for simple amusement or pleasure. Nor is it for those who regard ideas as puzzles for the entertainment of empty-minded people standing on a margin of life.

Quaddafi's ideas interpret life as it erupts from the hearts of the tormented, the oppressed, the deprived and conflicting reality in search of whatever is best and most beautiful.

Part one of *The Green Book* heralds the starts of the era of the Jamahiriyas (state of the masses).

Part Two inaugurates an international economic revolution which away with the old economic structure and brings them down on the heads of exploiters.

Part Three of *The Green Book* launches the social revolution. It presents the genuine interpretation of history, the solution of man's struggle in life and the unsolved problem of man and woman. Equally it tackles the problem of the minorities and the blacks in order to lay down the sound principles of social life for all mankind.

The living philosophy is inseparable from life itself and erupts from its essence. It is the philosophy of Muammar Quaddafi." Back cover; The Green Book, by Muammar Quaddafi.

He even advocates a chapter in his book about the slavery of black people. Let us go into it, Quaddafi says, "The latest age slavery has been the enslavement of Blacks by White people. The memory of this age will persist in the thinking of Black people until they have vindicated themselves." He continues on how, "This tragic and historic event, the resulting bitter feeling, and the yearning for the vindication of a whole race, constitute a psychological motivation of Black people to vengeance and triumph that cannot be disregarded. In addition, the inevitable cycle of social history, which includes the Yellow peoples domination of the world when it marched from Asia, and the White peoples carrying out a wide-ranging colonialist movement covering all the continents of the world, is now giving way to the re-emergence of Black people." Ibid, p. 121. Thus, he knows that we are superior, not just due to slavery but, "Black people are now in a very backward social situation, but such backwardness works to bring about their numerical superiority because their low standard of living has shielded them from methods of birth control and family planning. Also, their old social traditions place no limit on marriages, leading to their accelerated growth. The population of other races has decreased because of birth control, restrictions on marriage, and constant occupation in work, unlike the Blacks, who tend to be less obsessive about work in a climate which is continuously hot."

So, you see our Blueprint is to multiply and establish the kingdom of God on the earth, and remember that kingdom is right in you, so the black man must establish himself on the earth and build their social equality, like Marcus Garvey had advocated, "Let the Negro [sic] accumulate wealth." But many of our weakness holds us back, which is self-hatred, jealousy, mistrust of ourselves and thinking that every other nationalities or ethnic groups' merchandise is better than ours. In the book Marcus Garvey and the Vision of Africa, it says, "There is no doubt that the Negro [sic] is his own greatest enemy. He is jealous of himself, envious and covetous. This accounts for most of our failure in business and in other things." P. 141. Emphasis is mines. How are we to elevate our social equality if you cannot trust your black brothers? There are contract that can be formed to state exactly what must be done, and let us stimulate our own economy. Advocate our group of men for one common cause. Equality is distribution of wealth and goods. It means to share. So, why not Build and Destroy? By building our own we destroy the devil by taking away his business. He will get his part as well through the tax, unless we take the land that we want and become the natural rulers of the said part. And this is realism.

All this is was written, but Elijah taught that his guidance will not come from a book, yet directly from the mouth of God. **Jeremiah 31:33** says: "But this shall be the covenant that I will make with the house of Israel; after those days, saith the Lord, I will put my law in their inward parts, and **write it in their hearts**; and will be their God, and they shall be my people."— (King James Version (KJV)). In the past, they used to say, "No man has seen God at anytime." (John 1:18). But that is because of Yacub's grafted devils, but Moses and Jacob, and the peace maker has seen God. But in the in the world of the colored man, he had to teach you that God is a righteous unseen being somewhere in space, to conceal the true and living God, who is the Son of Man, Supreme Being black man from Asia. Although, he did not need a book, but all the activities with him and Fard was written and predicted exactly at the time that was expected and fits them to a science.

Moses was spoken by the Lord "**face to face, as a man speaketh unto his friend.**" [Exodus 33:11] Jacob called the name of the place ***Peniel***, and says, **"For I have seen God face to face, and my life is preserved."** Exodus 24:10, says, **"And they saw the God of Israel: and there was under his feet as it were a paved work of a sapphire stone, and as it were the body of heaven in his clearness."** Thus, if God appeared unto these prophets, then Elijah is the one like unto Moses. Jehovah made Moses a God. Fard made Elijah a God who would raise up the sons and fathers and turn their hearts towards each other, where for the first time in our history of North America you will hear the "***New Song***", "I'm Black and I'm Proud". This is also written in the book. All 144,000 of us will sing this. And we definitely see God, because we understand ourselves. This is why we are the nation of Gods and earths, NGE or NOGE, also civilized people, also Muslims and Muslim Sons, (5%). 1 John 4:20, "**If a man say, I love God, and hateth his brother, he is a liar: for he that loveth not his brother whom he hath seen, how can he love God whom he hath not seen**?" For ***Peniel*** means Face of God. Thus, God has a face, mouth, eyes, ears, nostrils, feet, body; Arm, leg; leg; arm; head= Allah. God spoke to Moses directly, and spoke to Elijah Muhammad directly. They erroneously credit Moses of writing the Bible, but that is dubious. Thus, the bible tells us that Moses was learnt in Egyptian Science. Thus, this is for the so-called Jews and Christians to prove, since the Sunnis are in agreement that the Bible was not written by Moses. Rather many biblical scholars or theologians admit the books were not Moses' writings nor did they belong to him. Otherwise, they were not recorded by him if he was able to elaborate his death and tell us what age that he departed from the time-space world.

Thus, black nation do not think that you are of little worth, since the educated mind sees and comprehends your situations. Why would Qaddafi write a book and speak on our condition out of random? He said we ***would prevail in the world.*** That is the name of the Chapter of his book, the 121st page. So, you see it is all mathematical and even the president of the United States of America;

Barack H. Obama had to address the racial intensity in his government of whites and the legislature. He said he experienced the same treatments that black people are receiving in European power structures. So, America have serious problem. The problem of America is like the record says, "Self-destruction, you headed for self-destruction." Black people are headed for self-destruction if they keep feeling inferior to other people (Caucasians), and white people are headed for destruction thinking that they are superior to everyone else other than their own people. You can start seeing their destructions now. America has been experiencing lots of storms and calamity; lots of fires that has been caused by lightning that has been burning many homes and it's a continuous cycle of this type of phenomenon. America is facing storm after storm, because it is all written in the Bible. Earthquakes and pestilence and rumors of war are mentioned so that you can know how the Days of Noah were and "So will the Days of the Son of man shall be."

So, Richard King wrote the book MELANIN: a Key to Freedom, and just by the tittle alone you can consciously detect that it is dealing with the realization of self. He says, "Please consider the 32nd of 42 Negative Confessions of Ancient Kemet, 'Hail, Serekhi, coming forth from Unth, 'I have not . . . my skin, I have not . . . the god.' (Budge E. A. W., Osiris, The Egyptian Religion of Ressurection, University Books, New Hyde Park, New York, pp. 342, 1961). The importance of skin was so important to Kamites, whose skin was Black from high levels of eumelanin, that proper treatment of the skin was specifically listed as one of the 42 Negative Confessions for development of the Heart, Will, and Right Cortical Consciousness. Dr. Patricia (Sekmet) Newton in public communication (Baltimore, Maryland, 1994) has offered the interpretation, "I have not BLEACHED my skin." Page 71, by Richard King, M.D. Thus, let us not think that we should not be conscious about our skin colors. Like Job, "**My skin is black upon me**, and my bones are burned with heat." (Job 30:30).

Well, most of the prophets of the Bible were black and we can start from the last prophets of the Jews, which is Jesus.

Revelation 1:14-15

His head and his hairs were white like wool, as white as snow; and his eyes were as a flame of fire;

And his feet like unto fine brass, as if they burned in a furnace; and his voice as the sound of many waters.

If one has woolly hair, then naturally you will see that such hair type belongs to Buddha, the Gods, Ancient of Days, Daniel and most of those the devils call Africans. We call this continent Asia, but the devil calls it Africa to try to divide and conquer the black nations. We are also called the Lost Tribe of Shabbazz. At the above, they say that his feet were like unto fine brass, as if they had been burnt in a furnace. Now, we know that is symbolic language and allegorical, since we do not know anyone with brass feet. They were not brass, but "Like unto fine brass" as if burnt in a "furnace". What is a furnace? Furnace is used for baking clay or pottery, like the ones discovered in Megiddo. Thus, when one put brass unto the fire, what is the result of the brass? It becomes black. And Jesus feet were like unto that which is black, and if the last part of his body is black, this also means that the rest of his body parts were also black.

Now, many will throw it out there and say that is your Bible and my Bible do not say that. But this is the King James Version, which most of the versions were copied from and this version was translated in the year 1611. It began earlier but was completed in that year. Just to reject the fact, because of the racial mind of Caucasians, they do not accept divine truth and you can tell his nature by his physical body under the sun-light. His physical being rejects the sun-light and causes their skins to have burns, and their skin begins peeling with sores. Well, this is how you can understand their nature, the devils' spiritual nature. They reject truth which is the light, and the light is the light of men.

This is why Jesus said, "Ye are of your father the devil, and the lusts of your father ye will do. He was a murderer from the beginning, and abode not in the truth, because there is no truth in him. When he speaketh a lie, he speaketh of his own: for he is a liar, and the father of it." (John 8:44, King James Version).

The Muslim and Christians say that Jesus had no human father, but if you ascribe God to be Jesus' father, then you have selected a person or a man to be his father. He is the Son of Mary, so he can be said to be from the Aaron family. And so this is why Prophet Muhammad 1400 years ago said,"O sister of Aaron! Thy father was not a man of evil, nor thy mother a woman unchaste!" (H.Q. 19:28). He was not calling Miriam Mary. No, he was just saying she is descended from their offspring. She is from the tribe of Levy.

In my first book Revelation of the God from the Ghettoes of Hell in the Body of the 5%, I have proven that Moses and his siblings were black. The proof of the complexion of Moses is proven by God in signs, "And the Lord said furthermore unto him, Put now thine hand into thy bosom. And he put his hand into his bosom: and when he took it out, behold, his hand was leprous as snow . . . And he said, Put thine hand into thy bosom again. And he put his hand into his bosom again; and plucked it out of his bosom, and, behold, it was turned again as his other flesh." (Exodus 4:6-7). Thus, if Jesus is connected to Mary, then he is connected to Moses, Aaron and Miriam, like Jesus, was like unto fine brass as burnt in a furnace. But since it's a lot of arguments saying that Joseph was not the father of Jesus, we just use Mary as the source; instead of Joseph who the nation of Gods and earth say is the father of Jesus. But John the Baptist was the cousin of Jesus, so we can use this to prove it. **Footnote #2481**, by Yusuf Ali sates, "Aaron, the brother of Moses, was the first in the line of Israelite priesthood. Mary and her cousin Elizabeth (mother of Yahya) came of a priestly family, and were therefore 'sisters of Aaron' or daughters of Imran (who was Aaron's father)." Holy Qur'an translated by Yusuf Ali. The Bible bears witness to the two being cousins by Luke, "And, behold, thy cousin Elizabeth . . ." (Luke 1:36). Thus, she is from the black family, she is also black; meaning her son was also black.

But Jesus asked his disciples who they thought he was, in the Coast of Caesarea Philippi and they answered him, "And they said, Some say that thou art ***John the Baptist***: some, ***E-li'-as***, and others, ***Jer-e-mi'-as***, and one of the prophets."

(Matthew 16:14). If he is compared to Jeremiah and John, his cousin, then you know the prophets were black, especially when John is six months older and is a Levite. But not only that they took them for a prophet, or one of the prophets, but they say he is Jeremiah, who said emphatically, "For the hurt of the daughter of my people am I hurt; ***I am black***; astonishment hath taken hold on me." (Jeremiah 8:21). Conclusion is that he is also black and can be proven to be black just from the womb of Mary. For Allah is not the author of Confusion. This is why the history and Qur'an of the original Man is the Asiatic black man, the maker, the owner, the cream of the planet earth, father of civilization and God of the universe.

Same way the devil tries to make us, black nation, worship him, they did it with Jesus; and the devil has no understanding of culture (Islam). He will not keep and obey the laws. Jesus said, "It is written, Man shall not live by bread alone, but by every word that proceedeth out of the mouth of God." (Matthew 4:4). But the devil took him up into the holy city, and placed him in the pinnacle of the temple, and Jesus warned them about going against and teaching against Allah, which he called a *temptation*. Just as the devil performs today he performed yesterday, "Again, the devil taketh him up into an exceedingly high mountain, and sheweth him all the kingdom of the world, and the glory of them . . . And saith unto him, all these things will I give unto thee, if thou will fall down and worship me." (Matt. 5:8-9). Jesus knew better just as the NGE and all the 5% of today, he said, "Get thee hence, Satan: for it is written, thou shalt worship the Lord thy God, and him only shalt thou serve." (Matt.4:10). Just as he come today and tells you if you act like a woman and wear a dress, black man, he will pay you lots of money. He is still trying to make you other than yourself. The devil is still at work everyday until he has been taken off the earth. As long as he is in existence, he will try to convince you he does not exist.

Matthew 12:18

Behold my servant, whom I have chosen; my beloved, in whom my soul is well pleased: I will put my spirit upon him, and he shall shew judgment to the Gentiles.

Who are the Gentiles and Samaritans?

The Gentiles and Samaritans are Greeks and Romans who were not obedient to the Laws of righteousness and this is why Jesus did not give the children's (Black nation) bread to the Greek woman who he compared to a dog. So not only was Elijah Muhammad given the knowledge of himself and his people by Master Fard, but was given knowledge of the enemies of righteousness. This is why the verse says my servant shall show "***judgment"*** to the Gentiles. And you know the Greeks are the father of European civilization, so the Greeks represent all Europeans, who are known as Gog and Magog. Thus, by going after the lost Sheeps in the wilderness, who represents the seeds of Abraham. Holy Trinity can be when the three great religions of Abraham seeds come together and bear witness to none other than Allah, Supreme Being black man of the planet earth. This is why you have the hajj for all people of the world to go kiss the Rock of Ages, God, and turn the people back to the original man (God). Not saying that the black Rock in the Kabbah is literally God, but a sign that all people must return to black man, who is Allah, the source and origin that made all people from himself. Like I said before in the earlier chapters, this is after six thousand years, which is almost the seventh, which the Jews call the Sabbath, and this is our Days, which is the Days of Allah and we must observe that Day and keep it Holy, and we know what Holy is. Holy is something that has not been "mixed", meaning no half-truths, "diluted", to diminish the value or strength of a cipher (person, place, or thing), or "tampered" within any forms. Tampered is altering the state and condition or existence of anything. Thus, we must not pollute our Sabbath. Seven thousandth year, after the devil has been put off for trying to violate our Days, with homosexuality, opposition of the true and living God and their different levels of grafted mentalities within the population of the planet earth. Russia even rejected such negativity and Nigeria do not tolerate this; and all the civilized nation behold and see the wickedness invading their population by the devil, colored man; or Yacub's grafted devils, who are Gentiles; and Christians, and Samaritans. Jesus dictated: "These twelve" saying, "Go not into the way of the Gentiles, and into any city of the Samaritans enter ye not." (Matthew 10:5).

Thus, this is the manifestation (wisdom) of the 4.4 billion black people in the world. Jesus spoke about this time and you can see it. He spoke the name of Daniel and many people do not know what that means. They represent the first, so they are the 144,000 thousand mentioned in the Bible, commanded by the 24 elders, who manifested the 25,000 years of Qur'an, which is 2:44 that tells you of the quote of Daniel, "And in the days of these kings shall the God of heaven set up a kingdom, which shall never be destroyed: and the kingdom shall not be left to other people, but it shall break in pieces and consume all these kingdoms, and it shall stand for ever." (Daniel 2:44). Jesus spoke of Daniel in (Matthew 24:15) and repeated the ***Abomination of Desolation*** that Daniel had advocated. Well, there are 5 different verses that elaborate this. Let us go into that.

Daniel 9:27
He will confirm a covenant with many for one '**seven.**' In the middle of the 'seven' he will put an end to sacrifice and offering. And at the temple he will set up an abomination that causes desolation, until the end that is decreed is poured out on him."

Daniel 11:31
"His armed forces will rise up to desecrate the temple fortress and will abolish the daily sacrifice. Then they will set up the abomination that causes desolation.

Daniel 12:11
"From the time that the daily sacrifice is abolished and the abomination that causes desolation is set up, there will be 1,290 days. (43 months=3.5) 3 1/2 years he stayed teaching Elijah.

Matthew 24:15
"So when you see standing in the holy place 'the abomination that causes desolation,' spoken of through the prophet Daniel—let the reader understand—

Mark 13:14

"When you see 'the abomination that causes desolation' standing where it does not belong—let the reader understand—then let those who are in Judea flee to the mountains.

One 'seven' in Daniel (9:27) represents God and he had already given you a vision of God with hair of "pure wool". Thus, let the reader understand. Now, we have 1-44,000—2-44,000 and 3-44,000; and that is knowledge, wisdom and understanding—man, woman and children. All over the planet 4,400,000,000 is the population of the original nation. All this is mathematically saying is that the knowledge of the original man (4.4 million) is to be knowledged, wisdomed and understood in the cipher. Let us go more into the time and the way of God.

Isaiah 1:1-7 (NIV)

1 The vision concerning Judah and Jerusalem that Isaiah son of Amoz saw during the reigns of Uzziah, Jotham, Ahaz and Hezekiah, kings of Judah.
A Rebellious Nation

2 Hear me, you heavens! Listen, earth!
For the Lord has spoken:
"I reared children and brought them up,
but they have rebelled against me.
3 The ox knows its master,
the donkey its owner's manger,
but Israel does not know,
my people do not understand."

4 Woe to the sinful nation,
a people whose guilt is great,
a brood of evildoers,
children given to corruption!
They have forsaken the Lord;
they have spurned the Holy One of Israel
and turned their backs on him.

5 Why should you be beaten anymore?

Why do you persist in rebellion?
Your whole head is injured,
your whole heart afflicted.
6 From the sole of your foot to the top of your head
there is no soundness—
only wounds and welts
and open sores,
not cleansed or bandaged
or soothed with olive oil.

7 Your country is desolate,
your cities burned with fire;
your fields are being stripped by foreigners
right before you,
laid waste as when overthrown by strangers.

For our land is the planet earth, we must claim all 12 trillion, 478 billion, 118 million and 400 thousand inches on our planet. And take guidance from the Messenger of Allah, and know that we are the nation of Gods and earth, regardless to whom or what so claim citizenship to the nation who is all wise and does everything right and exact. **Holy Qur'an 9:24**, says, "Say: If it be that your fathers, your sons, your brothers, your mates, or your kindred; the wealth that ye have gained; the commerce in which ye fear a decline: or the dwellings in which ye delight - are dearer to you than Allah, or His Messenger, or the striving in His cause; - then wait until Allah brings about His decision: and Allah guides not the rebellious."

If you know the teachings you are the messenger, and this is the duty of a civilized person; teaching science and the mathematical principle to resurrect the dead from mental death and power. Elijah taught also the black man is God. For he taught Malcolm X, Captain Joseph, Farrakhan, Muhammad Ali, Yahweh Ben Yahweh. He taught the father as well. So when Allah made it born in 1964, he actually brought all the temples within you and you became the rejected stone who is becoming head, the Rock of Ages. But it all began in Southeast, Arabia, at the holy city of Mecca, meaning the source of knowledge. The Muslim says that

Adam was a prophet, but I don't acknowledge Adam as a prophet. All the prophets came from the east. So, our history or Qur'an began 50,000 years ago, within the tribe of Shabbazz. But we got the wisdom that was originated by Allah in the east, which is where the Qur'an wanted us to face for fasting- praying to live to see the devil taken into hell in the very near future. Even if the devil gave up his evil ways it would be his destruction since he has given up his evil ways and Allah is most forgiven. He forgives whom he pleases. I forgive John Brown as a devil, because he rose above his people and fought for what was right and his name is regarded among the righteous for doing so and this is why he is in history and his name is remembered. Although, he was Caucasian, he has a place in the eye of the God of the righteousness. So, the black man of the east came from the Mecca and spread out in what they call Africa, but we call this continent Asia, because this was the source of our wisdom before we spread out all over the planet earth.

All the prophets from Abraham to Muhammad ibn Abdullah came from the east, which means that the east began having problems as well, since this is the root of civilization, and after the grafting and making of the Caucasians things began to change within the planet and started causing confusion among the righteous, until their being expel from among us, but some of the righteous ones that followed the law stayed in the land. They were what you call white Arabs, which were not original Arabs but grafted. This is a process which one of our scientist in the book of Genesis took control and ordered his people, "Let Us make man"? How? "In our own image, after our likeness", and give power to rule over black people for a six thousand year period. But as the land was multiplying with Europeans (Adam), he began to mix with the original population and since they were taught the teachings of their father Yacub, they began to multiply and push the original population out of the Fertile Crescent. "Now the serpent was more subtil than any beast of the field which the Lord God had made." (Genesis 3:1). So, they were within the part that they call Arabia, Israel and Egypt and Ethiopia. And that is part of the Garden of Eden. For this is the birth place of man.

Genesis 2:8-14 (KJV)

8 And the Lord God planted a garden eastward in Eden; and there he put the man whom he had formed.

9 And out of the ground made the Lord God to grow every tree that is pleasant to the sight, and good for food; the tree of life also in the midst of the garden, and the tree of knowledge of good and evil.

10 And a river went out of Eden to water the garden; and from thence it was parted, and became into four heads.

11 The name of the first is Pison: that is it which compasseth the whole land of Havilah, where there is gold;

12 And the gold of that land is good: there is bdellium and the onyx stone.

13 And the name of the second river is Gihon: the same is it that compaseth the whole land of Ethiopia.

14 And the name of the third river is Hiddekel: that is it which goeth toward the east of Assyria. And the fourth river is Euphrates.

Throughout the entire chapter two you can see the episode of the devil being birthed and placed in the east, where knowledge and wisdom of the original man first started. "And the Lord God took the man, and put him into the Garden of Eden to dress it and to keep it." (Genesis 2:15). The Qur'an also support this when Allah says, "O ye people! Adore your Guardian-Lord, who created you and those who came before you, that ye may have the chance to learn righteousness;" (HQ. 2:21). **"I will create a vicegerent on earth."** They said: **"Wilt Thou place therein one who will make mischief therein and shed blood?- whilst we do celebrate Thy praises and glorify Thy holy (name)?"** He said: **"I know what ye know not."** (HQ. 2:30). So God will place that vicegerent or put him to replenish the earth, or replace the black people there and supplant the black man's rule. And each people that came out of the black man, the brown man, the yellow man and finally the white man. Each taking 200 years. The yellow man put the black man out, and you can tell by Buddha that he was a black man living in Asia; and J.A. Rogers also speaks of the original Chinese as being black and learn their martial arts from the black man from the black man. Finally the white people were the last to be given a civilization and they had the knowledge of Yacub, their father which was devilishment: Telling lies, stealing and how to master the original people. So, they were Muslims, Jews and Christians. They all came spreading their habits among the people in the time of Noah and in Sodom and Gomorrah, just as today in the European countries. America is the first, just as the days of Noah, so it is today and remember Noah gave warning there will be a flood and the people refused to take heed and they were flooded out in the flood. Well, if you refuse the guidance of Elijah Muhammad today, it is the same circumstances. You have to accept this and save your life by applying the teaching and respect to yourself. Elijah, the promised comforter Jesus ascribed to his disciples. All this started over in the east and it came to the west, just as the coming of the Son of man shall be.

However, the promise of Allah is true and let me show an example of just how true it is.

> 6. And remember, Jesus, the son of Mary, said: "O Children of Israel! I am the apostle of Allah (sent) to you, confirming the Law (which came) before me, and giving Glad Tidings of a Messenger to come after me, whose name shall be Ahmad." But when he came to them with Clear Signs, they said, "This is evident sorcery!"
>
> 7. Who doth greater wrong than one who invents falsehood against Allah, even as he is being invited to Islam? And Allah guides not those who do wrong.
>
> 8. Their intention is to extinguish Allah's Light (by blowing) with their mouths: But Allah will complete (the revelation of) His Light, even though the Unbelievers may detest (it).

9. It is He Who has sent His Messenger with Guidance and the Religion of Truth, that he may proclaim it over all religion, even though the Pagans may detest (it).

Now on the 9th ayat (verse) Allah says he sent his messenger with guidance and the religion of truth, that he may proclaim it "over all religion", so it is not a religion and something higher than religion, which is a culture of God, (Islam). Islam is the way of God. It means peace.

Not only that, but CNN has reported that Millennials are losing faith in the Churches. **The Public Religion Research,** in April 2012, reported, "1 in 4 young adults identify as 'unaffiliated'" and continues, "55% identified with religion when they were younger."

Do you not see the promise being fulfilled and what do they start doing? They start saying "There is no God", which is the beginning of saying there is no God but Allah, which shows that Allah is giving them the eyes to see reality. They are tired of the pie in the sky teachings, so they coming out of the Churches and they do not want to hear the fairy tales about things which does not add up and backed by scientific facts. So they tell Elijah Muhammad, 6. And remember, Jesus, the son of Mary, said: "O Children of Israel! I am the apostle of Allah (sent) to you, confirming the Law (which came) before me, and giving Glad Tidings of a Messenger to come after me, whose name shall be Ahmad." But when he came to them with Clear Signs, they said, "This is evident sorcery!" Or they may say, *this is something made up*. It is all spoken about in that chapter of the Qur'an. So, these young people are turning to Atheist groups and starting to think independent of the European churches. It is not sound, but you can see that Islam has been prevailing in the world. For example, there are "1,387,454,500 Muslims in the world" and "2,199,817,400 Christians in the world".* However,

*2008 Encyclopedia Britannica Book of the year; figures rounded.

there are more Muslims who practice the faith than there are Christians, which is broken up in many different groups:

- *Roman Catholics*
- *Independents*
- *Protestants*
- *Orthodox*
- *Anglicans*
- *Marginal*
- *Unaffiliated*
- *Doubly affiliated*
- *Jehovah Witness*
- *7 Days Adventist*
- *Baptist*
- *etc.*

Thus, those are different denominations. Some even say they are Christians to get special employment in the labor force. But as far as Islam, it has been the fastest growing spiritual movement in the universe, whether you are Sunni, Shiite, NOI, NGE, Moors and anyone who deal with Islam. As far as being Muslim, many of my A-alikes (brothers in the NGE) will say they are not Muslims, but we are not in the sense that, we do not submit to the will of some mysterious God, but we do submit to our own wills and do not claim the mystery God. If God is man, then God submit to his own will. So, Muslim to us, like Islam is not a religion, but a science and we are God of it all. We cannot get away from this. If you disagree, then you are saying you do not exist. Allah has a will, and he has the will to master and remain righteous. We have to correct all errors by taking everything to the roots and master the culture so the whole world can accept us for who we are, God. It can be shown and proven by both books and remember there is no mystery God, so how can you bow to the will of a mystery God. You can only submit or reject your own will. But there's no obligation to say it, but I just have to show you a different way to master the lessons and they are right and exact. But you can only tell this to the wise, who can understand the point, and not those who are not ready for the high knowledge. It says this in the Bible, Genesis 15:14-15 (KJV)

> 14 And also that nation, whom they shall serve, will I judge: and afterward shall they come out with great substance.
>
> 15 And thou shalt go to thy fathers in peace; thou shalt be buried in a good old age.

Thou shall go to thy "fathers in peace", meaning in Islam. Back in the days when I was coming up there was a degree called "City of Mu" and it demonstrated the meaning of all this. The Qur'an even says that Islam is the way of God. Mu means *One* (Allah) and Salaam means *Peace*. That is after you received self-knowledge and the 1-36 tells you that, and it was the father who left the lessons for us. So, if he did not think that why would he leave it unchanged when he changed other things in 120° lessons? He changed the Caucasians being the skunk of the planet earth. So, why did he not change that? You have to science it out for yourself. He said, "We were not religious or holy", so this is the understanding of the lessons. He said we are Allah, so if we do not submit to our own wills who will? This is why Allah told Muhammad ibn Abdullah to Say: "O people of the book (Jews, Christians and Sunni and Shiites)! Come to common terms as between us and you: That we worship none but God; that we associate no partners with him; that we erect not, from among ourselves lords and patrons other than God. If they turn back, say ye: "Bear witness that we (at least) are Muslims (bowing to God's will)."

For those who do not understand, it calls all the people out to dialogue to show and prove who the true and living God is and when we do show and prove among ourselves who that God is, bow down to his will by becoming him, not no mysterious being somewhere in space, but a live human being right among us. Bob Marley in one of his songs said, "Know that God is a living Man", although he was speaking of only Haley Selassie, but all black man is God. It is a known fact in Egyptian days of antiquity. It's real knowledge and this is the classroom of God. The lessons could be shown and proven by doing extensive studies and analyzing the lessons and you will get answers to your questions. If Muhammad ibn Abdullah was a sign for Our Messenger Elijah, who was quote by Moses, Jesus, the Pharisees and Sadducees, then his disciples, then you know he was on time. The father was a wise man, because he understood Elijah being the Messenger and never denied that fact, as told to me by first born Prince and a few others that was with the father of the Gods and earths. So believe we had to be in the bible as well, since Messenger Elijah Muhammad was in both scriptures and this is no exaggeration. When Jesus was on the cross, who did they think he called out?

Matthew 27:46(KJV)

> 46 And about the ninth hour Jesus cried with a loud voice, saying, Eli, Eli, lama sabachthani? That is to say, My God, my God, why hast thou forsaken me?
> 47 Some of them that stood there, when they heard that, said, this man calleth for Elias.

The spectators thought he was calling Elijah, because everyone was expected Elijah and he did not come until after he met with the Son of Man, W.D. Fard. However, here is a sign from the Bible relating to the black man coming to the wilderness of North America:

Luke 15:1-32(KJV)

> 1Then drew near unto him all the publicans and sinners for to hear him.
> 2 And the Pharisees and scribes murmured, saying, This man receiveth sinners, and eateth with them.
> 3 And he spake this parable unto them, saying,
> 4 What man of you, having an hundred sheep, if he lose one of them, doth not leave the ninety and nine in the wilderness, and go after that which is lost, until he find it?
> 5 And when he hath found it, he layeth it on his shoulders, rejoicing.

6 And when he cometh home, he calleth together his friends and neighbours,
saying unto them, Rejoice with me; for I have found my sheep which was
lost.
7 I say unto you, that likewise joy shall be in heaven over one sinner that
repenteth, more than over ninety and nine just persons, which need no
repentance.
8 Either what woman having ten pieces of silver, if she lose one piece, doth
not light a candle, and sweep the house, and seek diligently till she find it?
9 And when she hath found it, she calleth her friends and her neighbours
together, saying, Rejoice with me; for I have found the piece which I had
lost.
10 Likewise, I say unto you, there is joy in the presence of the angels of God
over one sinner that repenteth.
11 And he said, A certain man had two sons:
12 And the younger of them said to his father, Father, give me the portion of
goods that falleth to me. And he divided unto them his living.
13 And not many days after the younger son gathered all together, and took
his journey into a far country, and there wasted his substance with riotous
living.
14 And when he had spent all, there arose a mighty famine in that land; and
he began to be in want.
15 And he went and joined himself to a citizen of that country; and he sent
him into his fields to feed swine.
16 And he would fain have filled his belly with the husks that the swine did
eat: and no man gave unto him.
17 And when he came to himself, he said, How many hired servants of my
father's have bread enough and to spare, and I perish with hunger!
18 I will arise and go to my father, and will say unto him, Father, I have
sinned against heaven, and before thee,
19 And am no more worthy to be called thy son: make me as one of thy
hired servants.
20 And he arose, and came to his father. But when he was yet a great way
off, his father saw him, and had compassion, and ran, and fell on his neck,
and kissed him.
21 And the son said unto him, Father, I have sinned against heaven, and in
thy sight, and am no more worthy to be called thy son.

22 But the father said to his servants, Bring forth the best robe, and put it on
him; and put a ring on his hand, and shoes on his feet:
23 And bring hither the fatted calf, and kill it; and let us eat, and be merry:
24 For this my son was dead, and is alive again; he was lost, and is found.
And they began to be merry.
25 Now his elder son was in the field: and as he came and drew nigh to the
house, he heard musick and dancing.
26 And he called one of the servants, and asked what these things meant.
27 And he said unto him, Thy brother is come; and thy father hath killed the
fatted calf, because he hath received him safe and sound.
28 And he was angry, and would not go in: therefore came his father out,
and intreated him.
29 And he answering said to his father, Lo, these many years do I serve thee,
neither transgressed I at any time thy commandment: and yet thou never
gavest me a kid, that I might make merry with my friends:
30 But as soon as this thy son was come, which hath devoured thy living
with harlots, thou hast killed for him the fatted calf.
31 And he said unto him, Son, thou art ever with me, and all that I have is
thine.
32 It was meet that we should make merry, and be glad: for this thy brother
was dead, and is alive again; and was lost, and is found.

The 32nd degree in the 1-36 English C lesson no. 1, "They wanted to go back to their own country, but could not swim 9,000 miles." But you see in the Bible he made it back to the father, and so did we since our Messenger was to turn the hearts of the children to their fathers and their father's to the children's. It is all our symbolic history, which is called allegorical. We have travelled 9,000 miles mentally, where our civilized brothers from the east can accept us. We were lost from home for over400 years and after going through the lesson, we are Lost-found in the wilderness. The fathers are going to equal our knowledge to the circumference of our children and equal their history and Qur'an to our own, so what the father is the son becomes, and they become one in mind, body and mathematics, that which was before the Alpha and will be after the Omega. And when you add 32+32 you are at 64, which is the year that Allah announced his nation. Our blueprint is to put this before the world so they can see the nation of

God in person, which is the only way God is in. If he comes in any other way he is inferior intellectually to man.

Ezekiel 34:11-17 (KJV)

11 For thus saith the Lord God; Behold, I, even I, will both search my sheep, and seek them out.
12 As a shepherd seeketh out his flock in the day that he is among his sheep that are scattered; so will I seek out my sheep, and will deliver them out of all places where they have been scattered in the cloudy and dark day.
13 And I will bring them out from the people, and gather them from the countries, and will bring them to their own land, and feed them upon the mountains of Israel by the rivers, and in all the inhabited places of the country.
14 I will feed them in a good pasture, and upon the high mountains of Israel shall their fold be: there shall they lie in a good fold, and in a fat pasture shall they feed upon the mountains of Israel.
15 I will feed my flock, and I will cause them to lie down, saith the Lord God.
16 I will seek that which was lost, and bring again that which was driven away, and will bind up that which was broken, and will strengthen that which was sick: but I will destroy the fat and the strong; I will feed them with judgment.

We are the original people of Israel, but you have Yacub's grafted devils. Israel is in the east. When speaking of Israel, this is where Palestine is and so is *founded in peace*, Jerusalem. Founded in Islam, is the same as Jerusalem and there was a king in **Hebrew 7:1**, called Melchizedec, king of Salem. King in the alphabets is the eleventh letter, which is peace in the twelfth Jewels of Islam. So, he is king of Peace. The bible tells us he is "Without father, without mother, without descent, having neither beginning of days, nor end of life . . ." (7:3). What is the said birth record of Islam? Answer: "The nation of Islam has no said birth record, has no beginning, no ending. It is older than the sun, moon and stars." Thus, you can mathematically put it together and be comprehensive to the point.

However, just keep in mind that Muhammad Ibn Abdullah was a sign of Elijah and he was given the book by us (Allah), so he can re-educate the people of the east, who has been given their last prophet, before the torch will passed to the west, which is the Wilderness of North America. Elijah is that man, who would be like Moses. Peace and blessings be upon you.

Other Books by B.K. Uallah

- <u>REVELATION OF THE GOD FROM THE GHETTOES OF HELL IN THE BODY OF THE 5%</u>
- <u>100 IMPRESSIVE WAYS OF THE GODS WITHIN THE NGE</u>

www.ingramcontent.com/pod-product-compliance
Lightning Source LLC
LaVergne TN
LVHW061250100826
845148LV00008B/1075